# You Don't Need No *Stinkin'* Stockbroker

## Taking the pulse of your investment portfolio

*Doug Cappiello, MD*
*And*
*Stephen Tanaka, MD*

Writers Club Press
San Jose  New York  Lincoln  Shanghai

**You Don't Need No *Stinkin'* Stockbroker**
Taking the Pulse of Your Investment Portfolio

Published by Writers Club Press
an imprint of iUniverse.com, Inc.

For information address:
iUniverse.com, Inc.
620 North 48th Street
Suite 201
Lincoln, NE 68504-3467
www.iuniverse.com

ISBN: 0-595-09287-X

Printed in the United States of America

*A simple, concise guide to do-it-yourself investing for financial security.*

# Dedication

Dedicated to Camille, Stephanie and Ally whose support and love made this book possible.

# Acknowledgement

The authors would like to thank Bonnie Monte for her expert help with editing the manuscript, and Carolyn Smith for her technical expertise. We also acknowledge Dr. Barbara Modlinski for her help in finding a suitable publisher for our work.

# Contents

# Preface

This book is meant to be read straight through, cover-to-cover. Its goal is to inform you and empower you to take charge of your own financial destiny. **Let's face it—you are no dummy.** Like anything else, investing requires training, education, experience and mostly common sense. It is about commitment and early sacrifice for later reward. It requires knowledge, but even more important, it requires tenacity. You **can** do this.

The book starts out with true-life stories of several people from modest backgrounds who became wealthy by using simple savings and investment principles. These are not CEO's, but ordinary working people who know how to commit to regular savings and smart investing, and who use these principles to improve their lives. We then provide you with an education in the basics of investing—sort of an *Investing 101* class—so that you can become familiar with the terminology and options available to you in stocks, bonds and mutual fund investing. This leads to a discussion of asset allocation, and finally a step-by-step guide to get you started on your own investment portfolio. We even touch on advanced, but relatively safe, techniques to use short sales and options in small amounts, to add diversity to your holdings, and some zest to the time you spend investing. In the final chapter you learn how to stay informed on movements and changes in the market, monitor your mutual fund performance, and make annual adjustments to your holdings to maximize performance and maintain your asset allocation.

We hope you will agree that this is a sound and deliberate means of getting started with what we hope will become a consistent and rewarding part of your life. Thank you for taking the time to complete our book, which is a work from our hearts.

*Doug Cappiello*
*Stephen Tanaka*

# Introduction to Investing

After many years of individual investing we've learned a great deal. Like everyone, we started as novices, fearful of making mistakes, and lacking the knowledge or experience to do things right the first time. As a result, we wasted money, failed in our attempts to time the market, paid overly high commissions and missed opportunities. But eventually, we started to get things right.

We began to focus on the long-term goals. We stopped trying to make a quick buck, and developed a disciplined approach to investing that we are convinced will work for just about anyone. Furthermore, we feel that our message is especially pertinent because we are not professional investment advisors, money managers, or stockbrokers. We believe many of these investment professionals not only have trouble relating to novice investors, but often have different goals for your investment portfolio than you do. We are both physicians, specializing in Ophthalmology. Like you, we work hard every day and don't have the time to also manage a complex portfolio, or do detailed research on every investment. We are not in a position to trade stocks daily or get involved in sophisticated analysis of multiple industries or companies to invest in. We believe most people are like us. We all want to be smart investors, but we want to develop a program that allows us to enjoy the long term results without the hassles and stress of personally managing an investment portfolio.

We began to speak with people about finances and found out some very interesting things. First of all, the vast majority of people, even with high incomes, know very little about the fundamentals of investing. They would listen to suggestions we made, mesmerized by what we considered common sense. Most of these people have the majority of their investment dollars in CD's or money market funds, which is a poor long-term strategy. By sitting on the sidelines, over the long haul, they have taken more risk by NOT being in the stock market. While they waited for that "golden buying opportunity," the market continued to rise, and their lost opportunity cost them dearly.

The second thing we learned is that many (not all) traditional stockbrokers do not have your personal financial security as their highest priority. The fact is that stockbrokers need to make a living, and many are placed in a position that creates a conflict of interest. After all, they make their money by placing trades for you. The more trades they make, the more they earn. Furthermore, those investments with the highest commissions are the most attractive to them. This is the reason stock brokers generally push high-commission investments such as annuities, fail to recommend inexpensive no-load mutual funds, and tend to generate high trading volumes for their clients' accounts. The cumulative expense of this type of trading style costs investors immeasurably, not only in commissions and transaction fees, but also in the potential growth this lost money would generate if invested wisely over the years.

At this point we would like to make a distinction. Like all investors we need stockbrokers to execute trades on our behalf—to purchase and sell stocks, bonds and mutual funds for us. This is generally done by depositing money in an investment account with a brokerage firm and using them as our agent. To do this we recommend the use of **discount brokers**. These companies simply serve the function described above and charge a small commission and/or transaction fee for their services. They also maintain your account records, provide monthly account statements and keep track of taxable events such as capital gains, dividends, etc. They *do not* make investment decisions for you. That is the realm of the **traditional stockbroker**. This is the group that we are concerned about. In this relationship, investors entrust their investment portfolio to a broker, who has responsibility for its performance. These investors expect the broker to make decisions that are in their best interest, and often abdicate responsibility for their own money. As mentioned above, the traditional stockbroker often deals with a conflict of interest that does not lead to the best outcome for the small investor. Many have been known to "churn" investor's accounts by frequently buying and selling stocks with high commissions. And of course there are the occasional horror stories, where the little old widow down the street lost her entire nest egg when her broker put it all on coffee futures. We admit this is rare and most traditional brokers do their best on behalf of their clients. However, we firmly believe that new technology such as the Internet makes it especially easy for individual investors to control their own destiny. It is no longer necessary to rely on a stockbroker to research companies or mutual finds. Anyone with a computer has the ability to do this on his or her own. And with the advent of **Internet based trading**, some discount brokers will execute trades of up to 1,000 shares of stock for less than $10. Compare that with hundreds of dollars for a traditional broker.

So these are the factors that prompted us to write this book. We believe you are yearning for a simple guide to investing that applies to everyone, written by ordinary investors using plain language. We also believe most people are wary of traditional stockbrokers. We offer an investment strategy you can pursue on your own, not only to save money, but also to maximize return and build pride in knowing you did it yourself.

So if you are a novice investor, interested in gaining knowledge and experience, and are willing to save for the future, this book is for you. We will inform you, educate you, and provide you with a step-by-step guide to developing your own investment portfolio using no-load mutual funds, low cost discount brokers, or better yet, very inexpensive internet-based trading.

We recommend you read the book from cover-to-cover. Each chapter builds on the next, as opposed to a reference book on investing. It is our hope that when you complete it you will feel empowered, armed and ready to tackle the complex world of investing without professional assistance. It is our goal that truly, you won't need no *stinkin'* stockbroker.

# Real Life Stories

You've heard the stories—the 82-year-old former janitor at the local high school dies, leaving a $2.5 million estate to the local library; the 52-year-old city worker retires from his job and sets out on a worldwide sailing adventure; or even closer to home, your best friend who never seemed to have any money, drove an old car, wore out-of-style clothing, and took few costly vacations tells you that he has saved all the money he will ever need, and has retired from his job a full 10 years before you could even think about doing so.

These stories are not fictitious, but are common and actual occurrences. The heroes of the stories are ordinary people. These are not people who won the lottery, or were lucky enough to invest in Microsoft or Intel before they became household names. Instead these are the people that we call the "savers" of the world. They were willing to sacrifice some luxuries early in life so they could make regular investments with the long term goal of financial security. In effect, their early sacrifices have allowed them to retire at a younger age, with greater security, better health, and more time to enjoy the fruits of their labor.

We were amazed when we read statistics that describe the life of the average American senior citizen. They are relatively poor, with few financial assets. Only around 20% of seniors in this country live a lifestyle better than the near-poverty level afforded by social security alone. Look at older people you know. Are they living the type of life you want 20, 30, or 40 years from now? What assets do they have?

Many do not even own a home. This is a disgrace. A nation this wealthy could easily provide a better retirement lifestyle. The real crime is that with a little sacrifice earlier in life and a dedicated investment program, most of these people could be living a life of comfort and leisure, commensurate with the decades of hard work they put in during their productive years.

This is the real message we are trying to convey to you. The financial markets of the world possess so much potential to build wealth that there is little justification for anyone to end up reliant on social security for their next meal. All it takes is a little knowledge, an ability to overcome the inertia that keeps you from getting started, and a plan that combines regular savings with diversified investing. While it might mean you won't be able to "keep up with the Jones's" and buy that new sports car every two years, we assure you that when it really matters you will have the assets you need to enjoy life, while they might not. We liken our message to the fable about the rabbit and the tortoise. While you might feel as if the early sacrifice slows you down, we assure you it is the best way to cross the finish line in first place. So, we encourage you to get into a positive frame of mind, concentrate on the long term goals, and read on to learn how you can take control of your own financial destiny without reliance on stock brokers, financial advisors or insurance agents.

# Categories of Investments

Before getting into specifics, we must explain what choices are available to you. First of all, the tax laws play a major role in investing. In this book we divide our advice into two main categories: tax favored accounts, and taxable accounts (also called "personal" money).

## Tax favored investing

You all know how large a bite the government takes out of our paychecks each month. Every time we get a raise Uncle Sam gets a cut of the action. The same is true with our investments. As we earn dividends, interest or realize capital gains from our investment accounts, the taxman expects his share. However, there is one salvation from this incessant taxation. Certain types of investment accounts are entitled to special tax treatment. Most are retirement accounts, which allow all earnings to accumulate without an annual tax bite. With the exception of the Roth IRA and Educational IRA discussed below, which allow true **tax-free** distributions, most of these accounts are taxed when the money is distributed at retirement. So, they are not really tax-free, but **tax deferred**. The key point is that tax favored investing allows significantly more accumulated growth than investing in a taxable account because all the money is left in place to grow and compound.

### Individual Retirement Accounts (IRA's)

Historically, the most popular of all tax deferred investment accounts has been the **Individual Retirement Account (IRA)**. This program allows workers to invest up to $2000 annually into a personal account held with a bank, brokerage house, or Mutual Fund Company. If the investor meets certain eligibility requirements, the full contribution can be deducted from taxable income each year. This form of IRA is considered a **deductible IRA.**

Beginning in 1998, individuals who participate in an employer-sponsored pension plan are excluded from making deductible contributions to an IRA, regardless of their income. Furthermore, even for individuals who do not participate at work, the deductibility of contributions is limited by income. This means a high income employee, without a pension plan at work, is ineligible for a deductible IRA. For 1998 the deduction is fully disallowed above $40,000 annual income for singles, and $60,000 for couples. This limit will increase to $60,000 for singles and $100,000 for couples by the year 2007. Even though they cannot claim a tax deduction the employee can still make contributions to an IRA. In those circumstances the IRA is considered a **non-deductible IRA.** The only drawback is that you must keep careful records of the non-deductible contributions made to the account each year. When the assets are distributed later in life, you will not be taxed on the contributions made to a non-deductible IRA, since after-tax money was used. You will only be taxed on the earnings in the account. Without complete records you will not be able to prove that after-tax money was used for the contributions and you may be "double taxed" when you withdraw the money upon retirement.

Regardless of the deductibility of the contribution, the growth in assets in an IRA is tax deferred. This means you pay no taxes on the earnings until you begin to withdraw from the account, usually after age 59 1/2. This lack of annual taxation leads to much greater potential growth over time since all money is left in place to provide greater compound growth. Instead of part of the earnings being siphoned off to taxes, all of the money can be continually invested. This is a great advantage over taxable accounts, and makes a strong argument for investing in an IRA even if it's the non-deductible type. It is also important to note that the IRS punishes early withdrawals prior to age 59 1/2 with a 10% penalty, unless the withdrawal is used on account of death or disability, or for medical purposes in which the costs exceed 7.5% of your adjusted gross income.

With the sweeping changes in the tax code in 1997, major modifications have been made to the IRA program. This includes two entirely new plans, which never existed prior to the 1998 tax year.

The first new plan is the **Educational IRA.** This program allows contributions of up to $500 annually for the purpose of funding higher education costs for minors. It is set up as a trust or custodial account, and the contributor need not be related to the beneficiary. Contributions cannot be made after the beneficiary turns 18, and the account must be fully distributed by age 30. A single contributor may set up numerous Educational IRA's for different beneficiaries. Likewise, a given beneficiary may have several accounts set up by different people. So a grandparent can set up a separate Educational IRA for all six grandchildren, and each grandchild can have an account set up by several relatives or friends. However, the total contribution to all accounts cannot exceed $500 annually for any individual beneficiary.

The best part of the program is that all distributions made are tax free, not just tax deferred like standard IRA's. The money in the account must be applied to qualified educational expenses including tuition, fees, books, supplies, equipment and certain room and board expenses. Distributions that are not related to higher education costs are fully taxed and subject to a 10% penalty. Furthermore, unused assets in an account can be transferred to an Educational IRA for use by another member of the same family if done before the original beneficiary reaches age 30. Also, contributions made to this type of IRA are not considered part of the aggregate $2000 annual contribution limit to all other IRA's. As with some other types of IRA's, contributions to an Educational IRA are disallowed for higher income taxpayers. Single contributors with incomes over $110,000 and couples filing jointly with incomes over $160,000 cannot contribute to an Educational IRA.

Unlike the Educational IRA, the new **Roth IRA** is a true retirement vehicle. Named after Senate Finance Committee Chairman Bill Roth (Rep.-Delaware), this plan allows eligible taxpayers to make non-deductible contributions of up to $2,000 annually. The contribution is disallowed for individuals at incomes over $110,000, and couples filing jointly at incomes over $160,000. For individuals who meet these income requirements, contributions to a Roth IRA can be made regardless of participation in a company sponsored pension plan. Furthermore for all taxpayers with incomes below $100,000 it is possible to transfer assets from a traditional IRA into a Roth IRA without penalty, although taxes will have to be paid on the full amount transferred.

There are clear advantages to this program, especially for investors who are concerned about contributing to an IRA that locks their money up for decades until retirement age. Distributions from a Roth IRA are *tax free* (not just tax deferred), as long as the account is open at least five years, and the distribution is made: 1) on or after the individual turns 59 1/2; 2) upon death or disability; 3) to cover the costs of a first-time home purchase. This plan even allows "non-qualified" distributions before the age of 59 1/2 of all *contributions* to the plan as long as the assets are held at least five years. Any distributions in excess of the contribution amount are considered earnings within the IRA, are fully taxed, and are subject to an early withdrawal penalty. This means that early withdrawals from a Roth IRA are both tax-free and penalty-free as long as distributions are only from contributions, not earnings. This is a major advantage to younger investors who can withdraw partial assets from a Roth IRA for any reason without penalty.

For individuals who are not eligible for either a Roth IRA or deductible IRA, usually due to income above the phase-out levels, a contribution could still be made to a non-deductible IRA. This program has not changed with the new tax laws. Keep in mind, the total contribution to all 3 retirement IRA's must not exceed $2,000 annually for an individual taxpayer. Also, the new law has more liberal rules for penalty-free early withdrawals from all types of IRA's. Beginning in 1998, individuals can withdraw assets from any type of IRA prior to age 59 1/2, with no penalty, provided the funds are used to finance a first time home purchase, or for qualified higher education expenses for the taxpayer, taxpayer's spouse, child or grandchild. The table below summarizes some of the features of all four IRA classes.

### Table 2-1: Summary of IRA Types

| Type of IRA | Maximum Annual Contribution | Tax Deductible Contribution? | Tax on Earnings | Treatment of Distributions |
|---|---|---|---|---|
| Deductible | $2000* | Yes | Deferred | Fully Taxable. Early withdrawal penalty if distribution made before age 59 1/2 unless used for first time home purchase, death, disability or qualified medical expenses. |
| Non-Deductible | $2000* | No | Deferred | Contributions tax free. Earnings fully taxed. Early withdrawal penalty if distribution made before age 59 1/2 unless used for first time home purchase, death, disability or qualified medical expenses. |
| Roth | $2000* | No | Tax free if held at least 5 years and age requirement met. | Tax free if held at least 5 years and distribution occurs after age 59 1/2. For distributions before age 59 1/2 contributions are tax free if held at least 5 years; however, penalty and taxes apply for early distribution of earnings. Penalty is waived if used for first time home purchase, death, disability or qualified medical expenses. |
| Educational | $500 per student | No | Tax free if used for higher education | Tax free if used for higher education. Penalty and full taxation if used for other purposes. |

* Combined annual contributions to Deductible, Non-Deductible and Roth IRA's cannot exceed $2000 in any given year for an individual taxpayer.

## Company Sponsored Plans

As you can see, the IRA program has become quite complex, requiring thorough knowledge and understanding of all options before investing. However, the fastest growing types of tax deferred investments are the **company-sponsored defined contribution plans.** These are commonly referred to as 401(k) plans for profit-based companies, or 403(b) plans for non-profit organizations. These plans work in a similar manner to deductible IRA's in that the money is deductible from current income, and the earnings are deferred from taxes until money is withdrawn. Early withdrawal penalties also apply. These plans are extremely convenient since the money is deducted directly from an employee's paycheck, and the program is managed by the employer. While most employers choose a large bank or brokerage house to act as trustee for the program, the employer maintains responsibility for choosing the available investment options. For 1998, a maximum of $10,000 can be contributed to this type of account. This limit is generally raised a small amount each year. Best yet, many companies will match some of their employees' contributions, making this investment even more attractive.

One trade-off for all this convenience is a relative lack of options. Most employers limit the investments to just a few mutual funds. Fortunately, strong public interest in retirement investing has prompted most companies to re-evaluate their investment options, and many are enhancing their portfolios. If your company limits you, we suggest you contact your benefits department and *demand* a better program for your hard-earned money.

Whatever investment options your company offers, we emphasize one thing—**invest the maximum you can in 401(k) or 403(b) accounts.** If you learn anything from this book, please remember this one point. Since they provide a combination of tax-deductible contributions, and tax-deferred growth with the possibility of employer matching of contributions, these accounts represent the best possible means of accumulating wealth. Once these programs are maximally funded, we recommend supplementing your retirement investments with a Roth IRA contribution if there are additional investment dollars available. For those without company-sponsored programs, the deductible IRA or Roth IRA are excellent choices, depending on individual circumstances.

**Annuities**

Another form of tax-deferred investing is the **tax-deferred annuity**. These are basically life insurance contracts that are purchased with lump sum premiums, and carry a cash value feature. The cash can be invested in different ways and can grow in a tax-deferred manner. For several reasons we believe there are too many negatives to make this a strong consideration as an investment vehicle. Mostly, annuities tend to be extremely expensive in terms of commissions, fees and management costs. These up-front costs can be so high that it may take several years just to break even. Second, even though contributions are not tax deductible, there is usually a very large penalty for removing any assets (even contributions) during the first several years. This locks investors into keeping annuities even if they desire other uses for the money.

There is tremendous variability in the annuity market. Some companies offer reasonably low cost products with a good selection of investment options. Combined with the tax deferred growth feature, it is possible to find a good annuity for your investment portfolio, but it requires doing your homework. As you will see in chapter 6, we prefer the use of low cost index mutual funds over annuities for long term accumulation of wealth.

One thing that has disturbed us greatly is the way many brokers push annuities on unsuspecting investors. They have a way of making their product look great on paper, using charts and graphs to illustrate their point. But most fail to show you the fine print, and virtually none disclose the nearly astronomical commission they receive for selling them. And that is part of the point here—annuities are usually actively sold, not so often by knowledgeable investment professionals, but by sales people who know how to make a pitch. Hint—if a broker ever recommends you purchase an annuity with assets in an IRA account, quickly excuse yourself from the room and run away as fast as you can. If you think about it, there is no reason to ever place money from a tax favored account, like an IRA, into a high cost, tax-deferred vehicle. The only one who takes advantage of this situation is the broker who will probably use the commission to take a vacation to Europe.

### Other tax deferred programs

There are also a few programs that are specifically designed for self employed individuals. They have their own sets of regulations governing them, and are more specialized than the plans just described. These include **sep-IRA** plans and **Keogh** plans. Generally these are set up with the guidance of an accountant or tax attorney and will not be described in detail here.

## Taxable Accounts

The funds you invest **outside** your tax-favored retirement accounts is your "personal money." Since the tax-advantaged retirement programs have limits on contributions, many investors must then place additional dollars into taxable investment accounts. Here the earnings are fully taxable each year. As your investments generate interest, dividends or other income, the government gets its share annually. This taxation dilutes the long term earnings potential in taxable accounts.

Due to these tax implications, your personal money benefits from different types of investments than your tax favored accounts. Specifically it is easy to see why investments that generate lots of income would do better in tax deferred accounts since the gains would not be immediately taxed, and would remain in the account compounding earnings.

There are several ways that investments can generate earnings. First, bonds and other fixed income investments pay interest. In this case the issuer of the bond pays a pre-determined sum to the investor, which is usually a percentage of the amount invested. For example, a $1,000 bond, which pays a 6% interest rate, would pay out $60 per year to the investor. Likewise, many stocks pay a **dividend** on each share of stock. Both interest and dividends are considered **investment income** and are taxed at the ordinary tax rate, which can be as high as 39.6% for the Federal portion and an additional 10% in high tax states like New York and California. This means a taxpayer can lose as much as 50% of interest and dividend income to taxes if the investments are held in taxable accounts.

But investments can generate profits in other ways. If a stock or bond is purchased at a certain price and later sold at a higher price, this profit is called a **capital gain**. For example if an investor buys 100 shares of XYZ Company at $10 per share, and later sells all 100 shares at $15, a capital gain of $500 is generated.

Current tax law classifies two types of capital gains. **Short-term capital gains** occur when an asset is held for less than 12 months before being sold. In that case the gain is taxed at your full ordinary income tax rate, and is treated much like interest income. However, for assets held 12 months or longer a **long-term capital gain** tax applies, which has a maximum rate of 20% for the Federal portion. This is a substantial saving over other types of income.

Of course, not every investment makes money. Capital losses are also divided into long and short term and are subtracted from your gains each year to determine your net capital gain or loss. Remember no gain or loss is fixed until the asset is actually sold. Therefore, if you still own a stock that is worth less than you paid for it, that loss is considered a "paper loss", or "unrealized loss" until it is made real upon sale. The same is true for assets with "paper profits." These unrealized losses or gains are not part of the capital gain determination.

So the tax laws have a strong influence on how you invest your personal money. It makes sense to buy assets that generate little annual income and hold them for at least 12 months within taxable accounts to take advantage of the much lower long term capital gains tax rates. As will be discussed in later chapters, we favor the use of index mutual funds and/or individual stocks for taxable accounts. These investments generate very little investment income, and are mainly subject only to lower capital gains taxes. Other things to consider in these accounts is the purchase of tax-free investments such as municipal bonds (see chapter 4). These investments have the potential to bypass all taxation, but in exchange, tend to generate less income than taxable investments.

## The Three Investment Types

Now that we have described the various tax-deferred and taxable investment accounts, it is time to discuss the different types of investments these accounts can hold. There are three main categories-**fixed income investments** (bonds), **equities** (the stock market) and **cash** (savings accounts and money market funds). We admit there are other sources of investment, including gold, rare coins, commodities, art, real estate, etc. However, these investments require much more sophistication and risk, and are not recommended for the novice investor. Aside from investing in our own homes, we own none of these investments, we do not recommend them, and we will not discuss them in this book.

### Fixed Income Investments

In the next chapter we will expand upon this important category of investment. For now, suffice to say that fixed income investments invest mainly in bonds. Practically speaking, these are loans which pay a relatively set dividend or interest rate on invested money. Of course nothing is all that simple, since there are many different types of fixed income investments, namely US government-backed Treasury Bonds, Savings Bonds, Mortgage-backed bonds, High Grade corporate bonds, High Yield corporate bonds ("junk" bonds), and tax free municipal bonds. Each has its own advantages and disadvantages as it relates to risk and return.

Since most bond investors are looking for safety, we highly recommend Treasury bonds, which are backed by the "full faith and credit" of the US Treasury. Theoretically, if held to maturity, it is impossible to lose money in Treasury securities, since the government can authorize the US Mint to print money, if necessary, to meet its obligations. In reality, no investment is completely risk free, but this is as good as it gets. US Treasury bonds also enjoy exemption from all state income taxes, although they are taxed at the federal level. Savings bonds are also safe, but generally have lower yields. Another excellent option is the "Ginnie-Mae" bond, which is backed by huge pools of mortgage securities. Other government-backed bonds include "Freddie-Mac" and "Fannie-Mae" bonds, which are less popular.

High-grade corporate bonds are also relatively safe investments, but require more homework on your part, since it is necessary to research the financial viability of the company offering the bonds. For this reason, we generally prefer Treasury bonds and Ginnie-Maes.

Municipal bonds are good choices for investors in very high tax brackets since the income they generate is generally tax-free. In exchange for the tax advantage, they generally offer a lower yield than taxable investments. In fact, higher yielding Treasury bonds often do just as well as Municipal bonds after taxes, but with significantly less risk. Stories like the near-insolvency of Orange County, California should convince you that local municipalities are vulnerable to financial failure, and with them goes their bond debt. All in all, municipal bonds are still good investments for personal money among high-income investors. Just limit the allocation in any one bond, or better yet, use a mutual fund, which buys hundreds of different bonds, limiting your risk. Of course, it makes no sense to place tax deferred money into a tax-free municipal bond fund. That would only nullify the advantages of this type of investment.

**Stocks**

We strongly believe that any investor interested in long term gains should have a sizable portion of his or her portfolio in the stock markets of the world. Over the past 65 years the stock market trounced every other investment category handily. In virtually any 10 year period stocks returned more than fixed income investments.

This is not to say stocks always perform well. In fact, there were some terrible spells where a great deal of money was lost. The market frequently undergoes a **minor correction**, which we define as a short-term drop of 7-10% in the overall market. These small corrections are not due to any major problem, and are considered healthy for the market since they drive out speculators and people who don't have the stomach for the volatility of stocks. Often these corrections are followed by a rally in the market where new highs are reached. Less frequently we see **major corrections**. In this case the market can lose 10-20% of its value over a relatively short time. These falls are more difficult to come out of and are usually due to fundamental problems with the market's value, or political or economic factors that may affect the market's performance. **Bear markets** are the most feared of all. In this case the market loses over 20% of its value, and the effect can be sustained, sometimes for several years. We don't have to remind anyone of the terrible years of the Great Depression following the stock market crash of 1929, or of the miserable long-standing bear market of the early 1970's when the stock market lost about 40% of its value. Even young investors are likely to remember the stock market crash in October 1987 when the market lost 22% of its value **in one day!** However, history shows that in every case, investors who stuck with it and remained invested were eventually rewarded.

The implications are clear. Your tolerance for stock market risk is directly related to how soon you will need the money. For those investing for retirement or children's college expenses, where the timeframe may be 10 years or longer, stock market risk is much less significant than for those saving for a new home this fall. Success in the stock market requires patience, a long term outlook, and diversification. In chapter 5 we will discuss stock market investing in more detail.

## Cash

We look at cash in one of two ways—either as the money you keep handy for your household expenses or as a depository for money waiting to be invested. For the former purpose it is generally prudent to keep about two months of monthly expenses in some form of cash account, in case of emergency. We recommend either a money market account or bank savings account for this purpose. These accounts pay a small amount of interest, are extremely safe, and offer **liquidity**— the ability to withdraw funds immediately at any time. For the latter use, as you will see in later chapters, we advise a gradual investment process when adding new funds to the stock market. The cash that is used for this purpose should be held in a money market account as you gradually invest the money. Beyond these two uses, we see little need to have any cash, since we don't consider cash a viable investment option in the long term. Of course, as you will see, in times of a bona fide bear market, it may make sense to significantly increase your cash position, but we consider this a special circumstance, and even then, we believe there are better uses of the money.

# Fixed Income Investments

Fixed income investments generally mean the purchase of bonds or bond mutual funds. Bonds are nothing more than loans made by you, the investor, to the entity that issues them. Since the law does not permit governmental agencies to generate capital through the sale of stocks, they issue bonds to supplement tax revenues. It is not surprising that governmental agencies such as the US Treasury, other federal agencies and state or local municipalities are a common source of bond issues. Major corporations also issue bonds to finance modernization, expansions or mergers, when it is not practical or prudent to issue additional stock. In all cases money is being raised in exchange for a financial obligation to repay the loan over a specified period with interest.

## Definitions

It is important to understand some of the major concepts and terms involved in bond issues. **Par value** is the face value of the bond, which is promised to be paid back in full on the **maturity date**. It is often the same as the price of the bond when sold initially. The interest rate, or **coupon rate**, is the annual rate of return paid by the issuer, based on the par value of the bond. The **yield** is the annual rate of return based on the price actually paid for the bond, regardless of the par value.

It must be noted that there is an active **secondary market** for bonds. Investors often buy bonds at their initial offering in the hopes of selling them later on for more than they paid. The company or government agency that originally offered the bond is not as concerned with the activity in the secondary market because they continue to make interest payments based on the par value and coupon rate. However, the secondary market has major effects on the yield of bonds. For example, if a bond initially sold for $1000, with a par value of $1000, and a coupon rate of 10%, the bond would pay annual interest of $100. However, if the bond was sold on the secondary market for $800 (assuming interest rates have gone up since the bond was initially bought-more on this later), the yield would be based on the new purchase price and would be calculated by dividing the annual income ($100) by the price paid ($800), for a result of 12.5%. Therefore, when bonds are purchased at par value, the coupon rate and the yield are equal. Otherwise, the yield depends on whether the bond was purchased at either a **premium** or a **discount** to the par value. In any case, the holder of the bond at the date of maturity will receive the full par value in return for redemption of the certificate.

## Backing of Bonds

Most corporate bonds are known as **debentures**, meaning they are backed by the credit of the issuing company without being tied to any particular asset. Other companies offer more protection to the investor, in the form of **asset-backed bonds**, which are collateralized by hard assets owned by the company, such as real estate or equipment. Some issuers even go so far as to guarantee repayment by issuing a second bond in which the funds are invested in US Treasury securities as a depository used to repay the first issue in the case of threatened default. Another popular group of bonds are backed up by a large pool of mortgage loans. Of course the safest of all bonds are those backed by the US Treasury. Since the Treasury has ultimate power of taxation, and even the ability to print money, it is considered a virtual impossibility for these securities to ever default.

## Types of Bonds

Other factors come into play when considering bond purchases. **Convertible bonds** allow investors the choice of converting corporate bonds into company stock instead of cash. Generally the rules for conversion are spelled out clearly at the time of issue. These bonds are attractive because if the stock performs very well, it makes sense to convert the bond, and enjoy the profit. If not, the investor still has the option to take a cash repayment, as with standard bonds. The convertible option makes these bonds less prone to interest rate fluctuations, and therefore, allows the issuer to offer a lower initial interest rate than with conventional bonds.

Another option often taken by issuers of bonds is to offer **callable bonds**. Simply put, this allows issuers to require redemption of the bond before the maturity date. Generally, bonds are called if the pre-vailing interest rates have dropped, allowing the issuer to float new bonds at the lower interest rate, potentially saving millions of dollars. Callable bonds are somewhat less attractive to investors since they can-not depend on a steady income for the full maturity period. They are less desirable on the secondary market for the same reason. To protect investors, issuers are usually required to wait several years before calling a bond for redemption.

Another popular option for issuers and investors alike is the **zero-coupon bond**. As its name implies, these bonds pay no interest, but instead are sold at a deep discount to the par value. Then, at maturity, the entire par value is paid off at once. For example, a 10 year zero with a par value of $1000 may sell in 1997 for as little as $385. In 2007, the bond can be redeemed for $1000, for an annual yield of 10% on the initial purchase. Issuers love them because they receive the investment dollars up front to put to work, but don't need to make any payments until the maturity date, often many years later. Investors like them because the deep discount permits them to pay much less money for each issue, so they can buy more bonds. They can also purchase these bonds with varying maturity dates, allowing them to time the payoff when the money is most needed. The biggest disadvantage of zeros is that even though no income is generated each year, taxes must be paid on the interest you would have received, as in a standard bond. Investors are therefore currently taxed on future income. As a result, we recommend only purchasing **tax-free** zero coupon bonds, or using only tax-deferred retirement accounts for purchasing these securities.

## Factors Affecting Risk and Yield

Generally bonds are considered relatively low risk investments. In fact, as mentioned, US Treasury bonds, which are used by the federal government mainly to finance the federal deficit, are considered virtually risk free. For this reason, US Treasury securities are ideal for older investors who depend on the income for their living expenses, and cannot accept any significant risk with the principal. However, as with all investments, risk levels for bonds vary greatly, usually in direct proportion to the yield. The highest yielding bonds of all, "high yield" corporate bonds, are often referred to as "junk bonds" because they are issued by corporations with mediocre or poor financial status. Junk bonds must pay higher yields to attract investors due to the very real possibility that the company issuing the bonds might fail to meet its obligations during an economic downturn. In this case, bondholders may be forced to await a long bankruptcy process before receiving any of their funds, or may even lose the entire investment.

Another factor affecting the yield of bonds is the tax status. The most tax-favored of all are municipal bonds, often referred to as "muni's." These bonds are issued either by states or local municipalities to finance public works projects, school districts, hospitals, etc. Most Muni's are blessed with a tax-exempt status, meaning the income they generate is completely free of federal, state, and even local income tax. They are extremely attractive as sources of income to individuals in high tax brackets, and/or those who live in areas with high state and local income taxes such as California or New York. In order to take advantage of the state tax exemption, the investor must live in the state issuing the bonds. Of course, this tax advantage comes at a price in that Muni's pay about the lowest interest rate of all types of bonds.

US Treasury securities also enjoy tax exemption from state and local income tax, but are subject to federal income taxes. This is true of all types of US Treasury securities, including short term T-Bills (maturities of 3 months to 1 year), intermediate term Treasury Notes (2-10 years), long term Treasury Bonds (over 10 years), and US Savings Bonds as well. This tax advantage, coupled with the guaranteed level of safety, also tend to reduce the yield on this category of investment.

Corporate bonds, as their name implies, are issued by major corporations to generate capital as an alternative to borrowing from banks or issuing publicly traded stocks. These bonds are fully taxable at both the federal and state level. The degree of risk is related to the financial strength of the underlying company, and this creates more uncertainty than investments in the US government. The risk rating is studied by several agencies including Standard & Poor's, and Moody's, which rates bonds on numerous indicators using an A-D system similar to grades in school. Generally, any bond that receives a "B" or lower grade is considered below investment grade, and classified as a junk bond. Highly rated corporate bonds are extremely safe, though not guaranteed, and pay higher yields than most government-issued bonds. Any individual investor interested in corporate bonds would be well advised to invest only in bonds rated "A" or better to reduce credit-risk exposure.

The last type of bond to consider is the mortgage-backed variety, of which the "Ginnie Mae" bond issued by the Government National Mortgage Association (GNMA), is the most popular. These bonds invest in the purchase of large pools of home mortgages, and receive income as these mortgages are paid off. In general they pay good rates of return, but are fully taxable. The payments received are self-amortized, i.e. they include both interest and principal with no lump sum payment at maturity. These are very safe investments, which should be a part of the portfolio of most investors.

## The Role of the Secondary Market

Most novice investors consider the bond market to be very confusing, and they are right. The confusion is caused by the large number of different types of bond issues, and by the active secondary market for bonds. Since most bonds have very long maturities, as long as 30 years or more, many investors do not expect to hold them to maturity, but instead hope to sell their bonds at a profit. Their success depends on the prevailing interest rates, and the effects of inflation. The confusion comes from the fact that as rates go up, bonds prices actually tend to go down. Intuitively this makes little sense, until you consider what is happening in the bond's secondary market. An example will greatly help explain this.

*Assume in 1994 you purchased a 30 year US Treasury bond paying an interest rate of 6%, at a price of $10,000. Three years later you wish to sell your bond in the secondary market. Unfortunately, prevailing interest rates are now up to 8%, meaning an investor can purchase a $10,000 bond directly from the Treasury, which yields 8% interest. Of course, no one would be willing to pay $10,000 for your 6% bond, but would purchase it at a steep discount. Since your bond is paying $600 per year, you would need to sell it for $7500 to insure the purchaser of the bond an 8% rate of return. This would represent a 25% capital loss to you. Of course if you hold your bond to maturity you will be guaranteed to receive $600 in interest every year, as well as your full $10,000 principal payment in the year 2024.*

*You can see how the opposite would be true for situations in which the interest rates have dropped since your purchase. If you buy a $10,000 bond in 1994 paying 8%, and sell it in 1997 when prevailing rates have dropped to 6%, your bond can be sold at a premium. An investor who purchases your bond would have to pay $13,333 to receive the same 6% yield to match* *the prevailing rates. While you may not receive the full premium, chances are you could still see a capital gain of around 30% on your bond, and this is in addition to the $800 per year interest you have been receiving.*

This example illustrates the inverse relationship between interest rates and bond prices. The longer the maturity of the bonds, the greater the volatility due to the long time horizon and the greater activity in the secondary market. It is for this reason that most money market funds utilize very short-term instruments such as 3-month Treasury Bills to provide maximum consistency in price with minimal volatility. Similar secondary trading occurs in other bond markets, making individual issue bonds somewhat complex for the individual investor, unless he or she intends to hold the bond to maturity.

## Bond Mutual Funds

For this reason we strongly recommend the use of bond mutual funds for the fixed income portion of your portfolio. Mutual funds will be described in a later chapter in more detail. However, in brief, the advantages include professional management, diversity, and low cost. The fund manager uses the huge pooled assets of the fund to purchase hundreds of bond issues on behalf of the investors, and has a full time team of experts who study market conditions and who make buy and sell decisions in an attempt to maximize return. Of course the bonds held by the fund continue to pay interest which is distributed to investors, but the fund price fluctuates on the basis of many factors, including interest rate changes, inflation, availability of capital, or even the expectation of a change in any of these factors.

## Treasury Notes

Aside from bond funds, we also recommend purchase of intermediate term Treasury Notes of around five year maturities. These can be purchased directly from the local Federal Reserve Bank, using a **Treasury Direct** account. This minimizes the cost of the purchase. If you already have a brokerage account set up, the Treasury Notes can be purchased there, but a small commission will be charged. Either way, we believe Five Year T-Notes represent an excellent fixed income investment that investors can hold until maturity and take advantage of the safety and state tax exemption of US Treasury securities.

# Investing In the Stock Market

## Stock Offerings

Unlike bonds, stocks represent true ownership of the issuing company. As corporations grow and prosper they often outstrip the cash capacity of the private investors that got them started. Since new companies are not sufficiently established to attract bond investors, most turn to the stock market to generate capital. When this decision is made companies obtain the help of an **investment banker** who establishes a price for the company's shares and offers them for sale through an **initial public offering (IPO)**. As of late IPO's have been fabulously successful, often generating tens of millions of dollars or more for companies viewed as having fantastic growth potential. Even lackluster companies can generate huge sums of capital in this manner. In exchange for this cash, the company must give up autonomy and control, since the stockholders are now owners of the company and expect a reasonable return on their investment. Stockholders must approve major decisions made by the company, including election of the Board of Directors, issuing of new shares, and decisions regarding the sale of the company. This is very different than bondholders who have no say in company policy. However, unlike bondholders, stockholders have no promise of any income or return of capital in exchange for their investment.

Sometimes companies sell additional shares of stock to raise more capital. These are called **secondary offerings**. In general, stockholders are unhappy when secondary offerings occur because the additional shares "dilute" the value of their current holdings. Since the company still has the same market value, the additional shares serve to lower the price of the original shares. For this reason, companies are reluctant to perform secondary offerings unless the price of the stock is very high and current stockholders have already been amply rewarded. We sometimes see secondary offerings occur when the company is considering the purchase of another company, and the additional shares are used to buy that company's shares of stock. In this case the shares can be used directly in a **stock offer**, in which shares from the purchasing company can be used to trade for shares in the company being acquired. Of course, a cash **offer** be can also be made, in which no shares of stock change hands, but the stock of the company being acquired is purchased for a pre-determined price.

## Definitions

Most publicly traded stock is in the form of **common stock**. These are ownership shares in which investors expect to be rewarded with price appreciation if the company prospers. If dividends are paid, shareholders expect increased dividends to coincide with increased profits. Of course, investors in common stock also understand that if the company performs poorly, their total investment is at risk. A much less popular type of stock certificate is the **Preferred Stock**. This also represents an ownership share, but unlike common stock, dividends are guaranteed and paid before dividends of common stock. But dividends do not increase if the company is profitable, and the price of preferred stock appreciates more slowly. Due to their preferred status, these investors are also more likely to get some of their investment back if the company fails. The net effect of purchasing preferred stock is that both investor risk and reward are reduced.

Like bonds, the real action in stocks is in the **secondary market**. After the initial offering, stocks are bought and sold by traders on the active exchanges. The company that offered the initial shares of stock plays no role in this process. If the IPO price of a stock is $10 that's what the company receives. If the stock price doubles, the investor who bought the stock makes the profit, not the company.

Fluctuations in stock price are generally related to investors' belief that the company will grow and prosper. Large companies that are well capitalized usually reward stockholders by distributing profits through quarterly dividends. These investments are considered **income stocks**. Small companies that are in the rapid growth stage cannot afford to distribute dividends, but must re-invest profits into the company. These stocks are considered **growth stocks**. Investors in growth stocks forfeit dividends on the hope that the company will grow rapidly, driving up the price of the stock. This will allow a profit in the future when the shares are finally sold. For investors who don't need the current income, growth stocks have many advantages, since they are capable of astounding price appreciation, and there are no tax consequences until the stock is sold. With income stocks, dividends can be re-invested, but they are taxed each year as they are distributed. An investor who bought Microsoft in 1990 and held the stock until 1997 would enjoy a 2,000% profit, all from price appreciation (capital gain) since no dividend is paid, but would pay no taxes until the stock is sold.

While this book is not designed to discuss all the intricacies of choosing individual stocks, it is helpful to understand some of the concepts and terms used. The most important factors to know about any company are the following:

| Price | The current cost to purchase a share of stock on the exchange |
|-------|------------------------------------------------------------|
| Shares Issued | The total number of shares available for trade in the market |
| Revenues | The company's total annual sales |
| Earnings | The company's annual profit or net income after accounting for all expenses and taxes |
| Book Value | The company's total assets minus liabilities |
| Market Capitalization | The company's market value, calculated by multiplying the number of outstanding shares by the stock price |
| Price/Earnings Ratio (P/E) | Current stock price divided by earnings per share |
| Earnings per share (EPS) | Annual earnings divided by Shares Issued |
| Dividend per share | The annual dividend paid per share of stock |

## Stock Valuation

Armed with this information, most investors can get a basic understanding of the business prospects for most companies. The data can be found in the quarterly and annual reports which every publicly traded company must generate.

Historically, a great deal of weight has been placed on the **P/E ratio**. This ratio allows investors to compare the relative value of stocks within their industry group. Stocks with high P/E ratios are generally trading at a high premium to their earnings, and on this basis alone may not be as good a value as companies in the same industry with lower P/E ratios. The problem here is that P/E ratios are fairly static measurements and don't look at the potential growth a company can offer its investors. A rapidly growing company with a lineup of new products and a P/E ratio of 50 may be a better investment than a struggling company with an outdated product line and a P/E ratio of 20. We believe the P/E ratio is helpful for studying large stock market indexes, such as the S&P 500 index, but is less helpful when looking at individual companies. By studying the historic P/E ratio of the S&P 500 and comparing the current ratio to the historic trend, investors can learn important information about the overall value of the stock market. The ratio may also be helpful in looking at very large, established companies, but is of little use in studying smaller rapidly growing companies.

The key is to study trends over time. Every annual report lists current and previous year's numbers. Obviously a growing company should show significant increases in revenues, and hopefully improvements in **EPS**, meaning they are becoming more profitable. However, many smaller companies operate at large losses due to the high startup costs. They will therefore report negative earnings and earnings per share. This is quite acceptable. The confusion is best cleared up by studying the projections made by analysts who predict the company's earnings in anticipation of the quarterly or annual report. The stock market often reacts either positively or negatively to these predictions. When the actual report finally is made public, the company can either meet analysts expectations, in which case the stock price will usually not react strongly, it could fall short of expectations (a negative earnings surprise), usually causing the stock to fall sharply, or it could post a positive earnings surprise, usually causing the stock to rise sharply.

Companies in trouble often trade at historically low prices. At this point the **book value** is helpful to know. If the company's **market capitalization** is trading near its book value, investors feel there is little growth potential in the company, and have traded it down to its net worth. Often these companies are losing money every month, and as book value falls the stock price goes down with it. Stay away from companies trading near book value, unless you are willing to be very speculative with your hard-earned money.

## The Major Stock Exchanges

There are four major stock exchanges in the United States. The first U.S. stock market actually began in 1790 in Philadelphia, but it was soon replaced by a group of traders who met on Wall Street, on the southern end of Manhattan. They adopted the name **New York Stock Exchange (NYSE)** in 1817. The New York Curb Exchange was formed in 1842, which later became the **American Stock Exchange (AMEX)** in 1921. While Wall Street has become equated with all US stock markets, many exchanges are not located in New York. There are five smaller **regional exchanges**, located in Los Angeles, Chicago, Philadelphia, Cincinnati and Boston, where issues from NYSE and AMEX can be traded. These exchanges are linked to the parent exchanges. At the close of every business day, trading results from each regional exchange are combined with the NYSE and AMEX to determine the Composite Trading results.

The two traditional stock exchanges utilize an auction style of trading. In this case, actual brokers negotiate face to face on the trading floor, trying to fill orders. The stock price is determined by the law of supply and demand. The exchange sets the rules of engagement but has nothing to do with the ultimate price of any individual stock. To keep things organized, a single company's stock is always traded at the same post, although there may be several companies traded at that post. Once a trade is made, the information is entered into the exchange's computer system for storage and verification.

Unlike the traditional exchanges, the **National Association of Securities Dealers (NASDAQ)** exchange is run by a complex electronic network that allows brokers to make transactions by telephone from their offices anywhere in the country. They can refer to their computer screens where constantly updated prices and trading information on thousands of individual stocks can be found. The NASDAQ tends to attract more growth-oriented stocks in industries like computers, telecommunications, banking, and retail. As a result, this exchange tends to be more volatile than the NYSE or AMEX.

The last major market is the **Over The Counter** (OTC) exchange which lists thousands of companies too small or infrequently traded to be accepted by the big three exchanges. These stocks are also traded electronically.

Whatever the exchange, stock sales will be based on the relationship between the **bid** and **ask** price for each company. The bid represents the highest price offered by a buyer, and the ask is the lowest price acceptable to any seller. If the **spread** between these two points becomes too large, trading in the stock tends to slow down. It is the job of each exchange to regulate the spread to stimulate trading.

## Regulation of the Stock Market

The Securities and Exchange Commission (SEC) regulates all the complexities of the stock markets. The SEC was formed in 1934 in the wake of the Great Depression, which exposed innumerable stock market scandals. The commission has several major objectives, and can use sanctions ranging from fines to criminal prosecution to enforce securities laws. Basically, the SEC is responsible for three major roles. The first is to see that investors are fully informed about securities being offered for sale. This is done mainly through laws requiring companies to submit quarterly earnings reports and to disclose all known information that may affect shareholder value. Second, the SEC monitors and attempts to prevent fraud and misrepresentations in securities transactions. The third main role is to monitor insider-trading activities. Insiders are people who work for a publicly traded company, who are likely to know details about the company's performance ahead of the general public. Insiders must inform the SEC in advance of any significant personal transaction in the stock of their own company. While it is perfectly acceptable for insiders to trade shares in their own company, it is not acceptable for them to use their advance knowledge to manipulate the stock's price, or "leak" information to friends or relatives before public disclosure is made. Insider trading activities are tracked publicly and can be an important clue about the future outlook of any company. For example, if insider activity shows increased net sales of stock, it may be an indication that bad news such as a poor earnings report is imminent. Of course, it may have no significance at all. You will read many debates about the merits of insider trading as an indicator.

### Leveraging Your Money

While most people use current funds for stock purchases, you need to know about the use of margins to leverage your money and increase buying power. When you purchase a stock on margin, you are borrowing up to 50% of the purchase price from your broker, allowing you to buy twice as many shares as you normally would. Your discount broker charges a fixed interest rate, usually ranging from 8-10%, and the loan does not have to be repaid until the stock is sold. It is quite simple to set up a margin account with your broker, which requires as little as $2000 in cash or securities, and is basically a contract in which you agree to repay the loan under well defined rules. For the most part these rules are established by the **Federal Reserve Bank** and SEC to help reduce panic selling during market crashes.

The ability to leverage your money is a powerful tool, as long as the stock's price moves up. However, it can also be very risky if you guess wrong. For example, if you purchase 200 shares of XYZ Company at $50 per share, you would invest $5000 of your own money and finance the other $5000 from your margin account. If the stock then moves up to $60 per share and you sell, you would earn a profit of $2,000, and could repay your margin account. Since you only invested $5000, your profit is 40%, less a small interest and commission paid to the broker. Better yet, the interest and commission costs are tax deductible against capital gains made in your investment accounts that year. Had you purchased only 100 shares with your own money, and no "margined" shares, your profit would only be $1000, or 20%. You doubled your profit by leveraging your own cash with your margin account. Of course, had the stock dropped to $40 in price, the scenario would be quite different. Now your stock is only worth $8000, for a loss of $2000, after reimbursing your margin account. This represents a 40% loss on your $5000 investment, compared to a $1000 (20%) loss if you purchased 100 shares without margin.

To make matters worse, the Federal Reserve requires that brokers institute a **margin call** when the value of the stock falls below 75% of its purchase cost. The margin call requires an investor to add money to the margin account either through direct funding with cash, or if necessary, sale of the stock. It is designed to protect the broker from investor default if the stock's value threatens to go below the balance on margin. An investor might be forced to sell a stock at a significant loss to repay a margin call, even if there is a good chance the stock price will recover. In our example, if the stock price fell from $50 to $30, the value of the stock would fall $1500 below the 75% limit, and the investor would receive a margin call. If he or she could not provide the $1500 cash, the stock must be sold to replenish the margin account. This creates a large real loss, compared to the previous paper loss before the margin call. For all these reasons we recommend against margin purchases for novice investors. However, with experience, buying on margin is a valuable tool and we encourage investors to consider margin investing in situations where the markets are steadily rising and the investor has excellent knowledge about a particular company and its industry sector. We also recommend never exceeding 15-20% of your investment on margin, as a protection against losses on the downside.

## Stock Indexes

One popular and accurate way to look at the performance of the stock market is to study various market indices. A market index summarizes the average performance of a group of stocks that meet certain eligibility criteria. Usually the average is weighted to the market value (capitalization) of the companies that make up the index. For example, if Company A has a market value of $2 Billion, and Company B has a value of $1 Billion, the weighting of Company A will be twice that of Company B. The best known of all market indices, the Standard & Poor's 500 Index, is made up of approximately 500 large publicly-traded U.S. companies felt to be representative of the general economy. This is broadly considered a "blue-chip" index because of the size and establishment of the companies making up this group. Since it is weighted, the larger companies such as General Electric, Exxon, Microsoft and Coca-Cola have a significant effect on the performance of this index. Other indices include smaller companies, or companies that make up a certain sector of the market, and give investors a more precise picture of the performance of various segments of the stock market. The **Russell 2000 Index** contains 2000 small and mid-sized companies. The **Wilshire 5000 Index** looks at the 5000 largest companies, and gives a rough approximation of the entire U.S. stock market. Because of market weighting, the S&P 500 makes up about 70% of the Wilshire 5000, even though it only accounts for 10% of the total number of stocks in the index. Other indices look at specific industries such as banking and finance, technology, industrials, and foreign stock markets.

A popular investment strategy is investing in mutual funds that track specific stock indices. There are many advantages of this strategy. First, indices generally contain hundreds or thousands of stocks, and there-fore, are highly diversified. Second, these funds utilize a "buy and hold" philosophy, purchasing the stocks in the index based on a weighted average of market capitalization. In effect, they can be managed by computer. This obviates the need for active management, and results in very low management costs. Finally, this strategy results in very low stock turnover, and therefore creates minimal tax liability for investors until the fund is sold. More about index funds will be discussed in the next chapter.

## Global Investing

One last item to consider in stock market purchases is the emergence of the global economy. In the past, the US stock market represented such a vast portion of the world equity markets, that there was little reason to look outside this country for investment opportunities. Today, the US market, while still the biggest in the world, represents just around 40% of the world's equity, and it is no longer prudent to concentrate an entire portfolio completely within the US. In fact the emerging economies in Europe and the developing world may represent a potentially better growth opportunity in the coming decade than the established market in this country. Furthermore, international investing increases diversification, especially if the overseas markets appreciate while the US market plateaus or even drops in value. For all these reasons we are very bullish on international investing and recommend a 15-25% allocation of your equity investments in this area.

However, there are numerous pitfalls to international investing. These include dramatic shifts in international currency values, unforeseen political events in other countries, and lack of knowledge regarding foreign companies' market. That's why we strongly recommend all international investing be done within an international mutual fund. More details on this subject will be discussed in the next chapter.

# Mutual Fund Investing

Since we recommend every investor hold 80-100% of his or her entire investment portfolio in mutual funds, this chapter is critically important. Mutual funds offer immense advantages, which makes them attractive to the small investor. These funds work by pooling money from thousands of investors, allowing the fund manager to purchase up to several hundred or more individual stocks or bonds on behalf of the investors. Some of the largest mutual funds have many billions of dollars in assets invested, allowing for tremendous diversification which would not otherwise be attainable by individual investors. Additionally, mutuals offer many other advantages including low cost, full-time professional management and the ability to automatically re-invest dividends and capital gains to maximize growth.

Most funds allow minimum initial purchases as low as $1,000, with subsequent purchases of only $50, making mutual funds affordable to every investor. If you think about it, what other investment vehicle allows a small investor to own a part of hundreds or more different companies for as little as $1,000? Through regular monthly purchases and automatically re-investing all distributions, even small investments add up to large holdings over time. For this reason, we recommend finding good funds and staying with them for the long haul. Mutual funds are not designed for short-term trades. Their advantages come with time, patience, and diligence.

Owing to the many advantages they offer, investors have flocked to mutual funds in record numbers. Until recently, only a handful of fund types covering US and international stocks and bonds were available. However, as the table below shows, most families of funds have come up with many different variations on the traditional themes in order to distinguish themselves from the thousands of other funds available today.

| Fund Type | Relative Risk | Investment Objective | Invests In |
|---|---|---|---|
| Money Market Fund | Nil | Safety with Little Income | CD's & Short Term Gov't Securities, i.e. T-Bills |
| Short/Int. Term US Treasury Fund | Minimal | Safety & Income | US Treasury Notes |
| Long Term US Treasury Bond Fund | Low | Safety & Steady Income | Long Term US Treasury Bonds |
| High Grade Corporate Bond Fund | Low | Steady Income | High Grade Corporate Bonds |
| High Grade Muni Bond Fund | Low | Tax Free Income | High Grade Muni Bonds |
| International Money Market Fund | Low | Income plus currency gains if dollar weakens | Foreign CD's & Short Term Gov't Bonds |
| Ginnie Mae Fund | Low | Income Dependent on Interest Rates | Gov't-Backed Mortgages |
| Diversified Bond Fund | Low | Income | Many classes of Bonds |
| Global Bond Fund | Low/Mod | Higher income especially if dollar is weak | Foreign Bonds |
| Balanced Fund | Low/Mod | Balance between income & growth | US Stocks and Bonds |
| High Income Bond Fund | Moderate | Highest current Income | Low grade "junk bonds" |
| Equity Income Fund | Moderate | Income with good growth | US Stocks paying high dividends |

| Fund Type | Relative Risk | Investment Objective | Invests In |
|---|---|---|---|
| Growth & Income Fund | Moderate | Capital Growth & Current Income | Stocks with good dividends and growth potential |
| Real Estate Investment Trust (REIT) Fund | Moderate | Growth & Income | Stocks in Real Estate Companies and Real Estate Investment Trusts |
| Value Fund | Mod/High | Capital Appreciation | Stocks with low P/E ratios but solid businesses |
| Growth Fund | High | Capital growth with little income | Stocks in companies with growth potential |
| Global Fund | High | Capital growth & International diversification | Stocks in US and foreign companies |
| International Fund | High | Capital growth & International diversification | Stocks in foreign companies |
| Aggressive Growth Fund | V. High | High Capital Growth | Smaller companies with high growth potential |
| Small Company Value Fund | V. High | Capital Appreciation | Small companies with low P/E ratios |
| Small Company Growth Fund | V. High | Maximal Capital Growth | Small companies with high growth potential |
| Sector Fund | Highest | High Capital Growth in specific industries | US Stocks in specific industries, such as banks or computers |
| Regional Fund | Highest | High Growth in specific regions of the world | Stocks in specific regions outside US, i.e. Pacific Rim, Europe |
| Gold & Precious | Highest | Hedge against | Stocks in companies that mine |

Table 6-1 Different mutual fund types based on investment objective

With such a myriad of investment choices available it can be difficult to choose the correct fund for your portfolio. Therefore, it is necessary to understand how mutual funds work, and how they fit into an investor's portfolio.

## Mutual Fund Types

In spite of the large number of fund types, all mutuals seek to obtain either current income and/or capital growth. Current income is generated through investments in bonds and dividend-yielding stocks. Capital gains occur when the stocks purchased by the fund go up in price and are sold at a profit.

Mutual funds also fall into one of two categories. The most common type is the **open-ended fund**, meaning there is no limit to the number of shares offered. As investors contribute more money to the fund, additional shares are made available for purchase. Likewise, if investors sell, the number of outstanding shares decreases. The price of each individual share is determined by the **net asset value (NAV)** which is determined by dividing the total assets of the fund by the number of shares available. With open-ended funds then, the share price is directly related to the value of its holdings. In some cases open-ended funds become closed to new investors to limit the size of the fund and allow the fund manager to remain nimble with investment choices. In these cases current shareholders can usually still purchase shares. Often the fund reopens for new purchasers again in the future.

This is in distinction to **closed-ended funds,** in which only a limited number of shares are made available for purchase, and these shares are traded on one of the major stock exchanges. Once all the shares are purchased, the price of the shares are subject to the same laws of supply and demand as any stock in an individual company. Therefore, the fund price does not correspond directly to the net asset value of the fund. Instead it reflects both its performance as well as the market forces of investor demand. Due to the unpredictable factors involved in closed-end fund investing, we recommend most investors stick with open-end fund investing.

Stock mutual funds come in many different varieties, depending on the **investment objective** of the fund. Some invest in established blue chip stocks. Others invest in companies that pay high dividends. Still others invest in foreign companies, or in just certain industries like health care, computers or banks. In any case, the main difference between buying a stock fund or an individual company stock is the diversity that can be achieved for the same investment dollar.

**Index funds** warrant very strong attention. These funds buy stocks that make up a specific, publicly tracked stock index. Since the stocks in the index are predetermined it is not necessary to perform research or detailed analysis on the fund's holdings. Therefore, management fees are greatly minimized, and more of your investment dollar goes to work on your behalf. As a result, index funds performed exceptionally over the last few years, creating massive demand for them. In fact, the most popular of all indices, the S&P 500 index, which tracks about 500 large publicly-traded companies on all the major exchanges, outperformed over 75% of actively managed funds during the 1990's. Furthermore, since they maintain a buy and hold philosophy, index funds distribute very little in annual capital gains. As a result, the annual tax bite is small and investments grow in a nearly tax-deferred manner. This makes them very attractive in non-retirement accounts. In fact, as we have previously described, the tax advantages of index funds make them an excellent alternative to high cost annuities. We strongly believe in index fund investing on the basis of their diversification, low cost and high performance. We recommend they become a large component of every stock portfolio.

**Bond funds** are actually quite different than investments in individual bonds, although they are both designed to produce current income. Bond funds have no maturity date in which your principal is returned to you. The fund owns many different bonds, all with different maturity dates and yields. Therefore, a bond fund's performance is based on the combined average performance of all bonds in its portfolio. As bonds mature within the fund, the money is re-invested to purchase new bonds, in accordance with the investment objectives of the fund. The interest paid by the individual bonds is distributed to shareholders, who have the option of receiving the cash, or automatically re-investing the money into more shares of the fund. The result is that bond funds generate interest income, like individual bonds, but the share price, as measured by the NAV, fluctuates with changes in the bond market. There is no such thing as holding a bond fund to maturity. However, bond funds can be rated on the basis of average maturity. Generally funds with long average maturities pay slightly higher yields but are susceptible to greater price volatility due to fluctuations in the bond market. This can result in greater risk to principle in long-term bond funds, and is the reason we prefer short to intermediate term bond funds for our income portfolio. In spite of this slight risk to principal, we believe bond mutual funds offer many powerful advantages to individual investors, and should be the major vehicle for the fixed income portion of your portfolio. Furthermore, bond funds can be purchased in taxable or tax-free varieties, depending on what type of bond is specified in the fund's prospectus.

**Money market mutual funds** are not considered investments in our opinion. They are simply cash depositories that earn a small income in the form of interest, while you wait to put the money to use in some other manner. Money market funds generate income by investing in very short term Treasury Bills, Certificates of Deposit, or short-term corporate bonds. They are considered nearly risk free, and aim to achieve a constant share price of $1. They only invest in the highest possible grade securities. Many are so liquid that they allow check writing and debit card purchases against the accounts. Like bond funds, money market mutual funds can be found in both taxable and tax-free versions.

## Costs of Mutual Funds

Probably the largest debate over mutual funds centers around cost. There are many ways that funds charge investors for their professional services. Years ago, before competition became fierce, most funds charged a **front-end load**. This is a sales commission charged every time an investor *purchases* shares of the fund. The effect is to siphon off 3-5% of the investment dollar, and use the money to pay commissions to the stockbroker making the transaction. Over time, the loss of this money in the investment pool can significantly reduce potential profit. As competition in the marketplace escalated, many investors questioned the need to pay such a high purchase cost.

This resulted in the increased popularity of **no-load funds,** which charge no front-end load, and result in potentially better returns over time. Since there is no evidence to suggest that "loaded" funds offer any advantages, we must recommend purchasing only no-load funds for your portfolio. In fact, the first thing we do when evaluating funds is to check the load status. **If there is ANY load at all, we don't even consider its purchase, unless it is a specialized fund, which has few alternatives.** Unfortunately, most investors who use a full-service stock broker have little opportunity to see the advantages of no-load fund investing, since their brokers receive little or no commission from selling this sort of investment. We see this as yet another conflict of interest by stockbrokers who make money based on the transactions they generate, and not by the performance they achieve for their clients. Some funds are sneakier than others, and have devised **back-end loads.** These are charges made upon *selling* shares of the fund. Although the money is at least kept working in the account until sold, we see no reason to accept *any* charge of this type, and we prefer only true no-load fund investing. One exception to this rule involves funds that only charge back-end loads if the shares are held less than a specified period, say six months. We believe this is an acceptable use of a load, since it discourages short term trading. If shares are held over six months, the load is waived.

Another sneaky charge is the **12b-1 fee,** utilized by about half of all funds to cover marketing and advertising costs. Since these promotional fees are not really part of the operating expenses, some funds feel justified in charging a separate line item for these costs. While we are tolerant of reasonable 12b-1 expenses, we still prefer funds that are devoid of all these extra costs. In this case we recommend comparing funds within each investment category to assess the range of fees, and try to find a fund that meets performance goals without undue charges.

The last factor in calculating the relative cost of a mutual fund is the **management fee.** All funds charge management fees to cover the salaries, rent, and other operating expenses incurred to provide investors with the advantages of mutual fund investing. It is reasonable to expect this charge. However, some funds take great liberties with investors' money. It is very important to compare management fees within each fund category to determine appropriate charges. As previously discussed index funds charge the lowest management fees since they have little need for active management or research. International funds tend to charge the highest management fees due to the complexity of this type of investment. In these funds managers must research companies in foreign countries, deal with the political climate and also work with fluctuations in values between the U.S. dollar and the foreign currency. The main point is to look at the total of all charges among the top funds in each category to determine appropriate charges for the performance being offered. For example, a no-load fund with no 12b-1 fee but an astronomical management fee may not be a better choice than a fund with a small 12b-1 fee but much lower management fees. Of course, this assumes a similar performance.

## Assessing Volatility

Many investors put their money into mutual funds to let professional investors make the decisions and do the worrying. While this is an excellent reason to use mutual funds, it doesn't necessarily mean that the fund will achieve its growth objectives in a straight-line fashion. Instead, like all investments, mutual funds often experience significant up and down swings in value, roughly mirroring the trends in the market as a whole. These swings are referred to as **volatility.** One convenient way to measure the volatility in a given fund is to study the **beta coefficient.** This gives a rough measure of the fund's volatility in relation to the market as a whole. The scale assigns a coefficient of 1.0 to the total market. Therefore, a fund with a beta coefficient of 0.80 would tend to be about 80% as volatile as the general market. A fund with a beta coefficient of 1.1 would be about 10% more volatile than the total market. One point to make here is that volatility is not necessarily bad or good. Generally a fund's long term performance is the key indicator. However, funds with low volatility may be better for investors with a low risk tolerance, or for those investing with a shorter time horizon.

## Turnover Rate

One last thing to consider is a fund's **portfolio turnover rate**. This is a measure of how much active trading is occurring on an annual basis within the fund's holdings. Funds with high turnover rates are very aggressively managed, generate higher costs, and need better investment returns to offset these costs. Furthermore, the high turnover may create more capital gains within the fund. These gains are distributed annually and represent a major **tax consideration**, which could reduce long-term growth if kept in a taxable account. In contrast, funds with low turnover rates, i.e. index funds, tend to have lower costs, and a much lower annual tax bite. While there is no hard and fast rule regarding turnover rate and fund performance, we tend to prefer funds with lower turnover rates for the taxable portion of your portfolio.

All of the information we discussed in this chapter is summarized in great detail in every fund's **Prospectus**. We encourage every investor to obtain and thoroughly read the prospectus on several funds before actually deciding on a mutual fund to invest money in. By doing so, you will become much more familiar with the terminology of fund investing, and will make a more informed decision regarding your investment choice.

# Asset Allocation to Meet Your Financial Goals and Limit Risk

If you are going to make your own investment choices without the help of a *stinkin'* stockbroker, the most important single step is to allocate your assets appropriately. This means you must decide how much of your money will be invested in stocks, bonds and cash assets.

Not only does asset allocation help reduce risk by diversification, it can actually increase your long-term investment performance. This is because markets tend to be cyclical and don't always perform in synch. While the US stock market may be experiencing a significant downturn, the bond market or the foreign stock market might be doing quite well. By owning investments in different types of markets, you can benefit from this asynchronous performance.

## The Time Horizon

Clearly, the most significant factor to consider is your age, which determines your investment horizon. If you are a young person just starting out in life with several decades to invest before needing the money, you are capable of accepting a great deal of risk. Generally this means you can allocate the vast majority (90-100%) of your financial assets in the stock market. With that greater risk you are almost certainly going to enjoy much higher rates of return over the long time horizon. However, if you are currently in your 60's with only a few years before retirement, it is imprudent to place more than 40-60% of your money in the stock market. The volatility of the market would create unacceptable short-term risk. The market may be down at the time you need to sell your stock holdings. Most of us would find ourselves in between these two extremes, and would allocate our assets accordingly. Remember that retirement is not the only investment goal out there. A 35-year-old with a child heading for college in 5 years might also wish to protect some assets by allocating a larger percentage to fixed income investments.

## Risk Tolerance

The second important factor in deciding asset allocation is your tolerance for risk. People are different, and it is not possible for every individual to follow a single formula for investing. Some people simply cannot sleep at night knowing their hard earned money may slip through their fingers, even if it is only for the short term, or only on paper. For this group of investors, stock market exposure is still crucial, but will have to be moderated so as to minimize volatility. Each individual must decide for him or herself the best balance between risk and reward.

With these factors in mind, the table below provides "ballpark" figures for individual investors. In all cases, you should only keep enough assets in cash accounts to maintain living expenses for about 2 months. The rest of your money should be invested as follows:

|  | Stocks | Fixed Income |
|---|---|---|
| Age |  |  |
| Under 40 | 80-100% | 0-20% |
| 40-50 | 70-90% | 10-30% |
| 50-60 | 60-80% | 20-40% |
| Over 60 | 40-60% | 40-60% |

In all cases, the investor who can tolerate higher risk should use the higher percentage in the stock market allocation. Risk-averse investors should use the lower, more conservative stock market allocation.

## Timing of investments

It is important to note that we do not advocate attempting to "time" the market, by trying to buy on downturns and sell on peaks. Virtually every investor who attempts this strategy ends up a loser. On the contrary, most skilled investors with long time horizons believe in regular, disciplined investments, no matter what the market is doing in the short term. By adding the same amount of investment money at regular intervals, a policy called **dollar cost averaging**, investors take advantage of downturns in the market by purchasing more shares of stocks or mutual funds at lower prices. Then, when the market rebounds, these increased numbers of shares rebound along with it. At higher market levels, that same sum of money purchases fewer shares of the same stocks and mutual funds. The net effect is to maximize your investment dollar, minimize your cost, and improve your long-term return. *We highly recommend dollar cost averaging with all new money entering the stock market.*

That said, we also believe it is unwise to maintain a large exposure to the stock market during a period of *extended* losses, in which the fundamentals of the market are bearish. These fundamentals are related to investor sentiment, inflation levels, interest rates, money supply and other factors that are beyond the scope of this book. Extended bear markets are quite different from simple corrections and can often last for several years, causing a 20-40% drop in the market's value. We don't believe it makes sense to dollar cost average through this type of extended loss. Even in strong bull markets, as has existed throughout the 1990's, healthy "corrections" of 7-10% are to be expected. These corrections tend to "cleanse" the market of nervous investors and those attempting to time the market. Once the correction is over, if fundamentals remain strong, the market tends to rebound rapidly and often will achieve new highs as a result. This is another illustration of the advantages of dollar cost averaging. In a later chapter we will describe sources of information such as newsletters, financial magazines, and Internet sites where you can find out what experts are saying about trends in the stock market. We will also discuss some strategies to protect your assets and even make money in bear markets.

## Make a commitment to saving

As you can see, proper asset allocation, combined with regular, periodic investment contributions are the key to long term financial security. If laid out properly, your investment portfolio should almost take care of itself. All you need to do is get started, stay in touch with market fundamentals, readjust your allocations once a year, and toughest of all, force yourself to make the contributions on a regular basis. In most cases this means denying yourself some of those luxuries you have gotten used to. But, you'd be surprised how easy it can be with a little discipline. After a while you won't even miss those little items, especially as you watch your portfolio grow each year. We recommend treating your investment contributions just like any other monthly bill. In fact, we suggest it is the first bill you pay each month. Write a check out to your investment account even before paying the mortgage, rent or utilities. Somehow you will find the money to pay your essential bills, but you might not have the money to finance unnecessary extravagances such as new cars, big vacations or fancy clothing. Furthermore, do not "raid" your investment account to pay for those luxuries. That defeats the whole purpose. If your portfolio performs really well celebrate with a new subscription to *Barron's Magazine*, not a trip to Italy. Compound growth only occurs when you leave the money in the portfolio. With time your lifestyle will modify to match this new financial reality. We promise you, it is the best gift you can ever give to yourself and your family.

# Using Options and Short Sales Safely to Enhance Return

By this time you should realize that our approach to investing is methodical, and emphasizes diversification and professional management through the use of mutual funds. Asset allocation serves as the underlying basis for all investment decisions, and serves to risk-adjust your portfolio to meet your individual goals. So why would anyone with this type of investment philosophy even think about stock options or using short sales? Hopefully you have asked yourself the same question. On the surface these investment tools appear at odds with a sound investment plan. Many people consider options and short sales gambling, not investing. In many cases this is true, but in some instances you can use these mechanisms safely to enhance income, and add another dimension to your investment program. Besides, it can be lots of fun. Of course, as part of your asset allocation, you would never risk more than two or three percent of your portfolio on this type of investment.

## Short Sales

When purchasing individual stocks, most people hope to buy at a low price and eventually sell when the price has gone up in order to make a profit. This procedure is known as **going long** on the stock. When you buy a stock long, you are expecting the company to do well, and this prosperity is reflected in an upward stock price. You are a shareholder in the company and your equity is tied to the performance of the company you own. On the other hand, investors who **short sell** a company's stock have just the opposite approach. They anticipate bad news, or poor performance on the company's part, which they believe, will result in a drop in share price. In this case, they don't want to own an equity stake in the company, and don't want to own shares. The beauty of short selling is that it is still possible to make money even if the share price drops.

To short a stock you contact your discount broker and tell them you want to sell short, let's say 100 shares, of a given stock. Your broker then obtains the shares of stock and promptly sells them on the exchange for you. In effect, you are borrowing the shares from your broker, allowing you to sell shares you never even owned. Once this sale is made, you just sit back and wait for the anticipated drop in share price. During this time, you are paying a small interest charge to your broker for the use of the shares. Usually the interest charge is not a major factor, since the expectation is to stay with the investment for a short time. Once the share price drops, you contact your broker again and buy back the same 100 shares at the new lower price. This is called **closing your short position.** The difference between the price you originally sold the shares for and the price you re-purchased them represents your profit, less commission and interest. For example, if you sell short 100 shares of XYZ at $10 per share, and then close your position when the share price is down to $8, you have earned a $200 (20%) profit, less the costs of the transaction. It is also very common to short an index such as the S&P 500 index if you believe the entire stock market is headed down.

Obviously short selling should only be considered when you have excellent information about a company. We recommend this for people who work in a certain industry, and who understand a given company's performance and market position very well. Even then, we insist you first do some research, review recent earnings reports, study analyst recommendations, and verify your information before committing any money. This is an extremely risky practice. Only commit money that you can easily afford to lose. If you are wrong and the stock price goes up, close your position quickly, take your loss, and move on. The situation you want to avoid is to watch the stock price slowly creep up, hoping it will come down again. Even worse, if the stock is heavily shorted, other short sellers may scramble to close their positions, resulting in a rapid rise in stock price. This is referred to as a **short squeeze**. In this case, you watch in horror as your losses mount, your interest charges mount, and you are finally forced to close the position with a very large loss. Remember, unlike long positions in which your losses are limited to the amount invested, short selling can result in almost unlimited losses if the stock price streaks skyward. So watch the shop closely.

## Shorting Against the Box

As you can see, short selling is a practice reserved for sophisticated traders and is not recommended for readers of this book. The main reason we introduced this topic has to do with a concept called **shorting against the box**. This is a much safer technique, and is very valuable for investors who have large paper profits in a stock they are holding long. In many cases it is not a good idea to sell a particular stock at a particular time due to tax implications or personal needs. But, if you desire to wait a few weeks or months to sell the stock, it is important to find a mechanism to protect your profit until you are ready to sell. This is where short sales can help you. Simply sell short the same number of shares you hold in your long position. Then, whatever happens to the share price, your profit remains intact. If the price rises, your long position increases in value by the same amount that the short position falls. Likewise, if the share price drops, the long position suffers, but the short position grows in value. In either case when you are ready to get out of the stock completely, the shares held in your long position are used to close out your short position, so it ends up a wash. Your large profit is protected until you are ready to draw on it, and your only cost is the small commission and interest charged on the short position. Shorting against the box is a concept we believe you should know about for selected circumstances. This technique can only be used for individual stocks, not mutual funds. Also, as of the time of this writing the IRS is studying this practice to see if it creates too generous a tax treatment for investors, so it is wise for you to check with your tax advisor before making any assumptions.

## Stock Options

As the name implies, **options** are investment tools that give you the right to either purchase or sell a given security at a given price, within a specified time frame. Rights to purchase are known as **call options**, whereas rights to sell are called **put options**. The key to understanding options is the time element. An investor who is well informed, and guesses correctly on the price movement of a given stock, can still lose money on options if the price movement occurs after the expiration date of the option. Although options are significantly more risky than standard stock purchases, they are also potentially much more profitable.

It is important to understand the terminology of traded options. Think of them as a sort of insurance policy. When purchasing an option the investor is charged a **premium**, and in exchange for this premium he or she is given the right to purchase (a call option) or sell (a put option) the given security at a certain **strike price** by the **expiration date** of the option. Since options generally expire on the third Friday of a given month (unless it is a holiday), the expiration dates are generally referred to only by the month. For example, an option may be listed as the September 20 calls, selling for $1. This means "a call option at a strike price of 20 which expires on the third Friday of September, selling for a premium of $1 per share". Options are generally sold as packaged **contracts** of 100 shares each.

We believe the key consideration in option trading is the relationship between the stock's current share price and the option's strike price, as they both relate to the expiration date. For call options, as long as the stock price is below the strike price, the option is considered **out of the money**. However, if the share price rises above the strike price the option has value and is considered **in the money**. Put options work much the same way except the stock price must be below the strike price for them to be in the money.

In order to make a profit in options, an investor must find the option adequately "in the money" to also offset the premium, and all of this must occur before the expiration date. A call option with a $1.50 premium that is $1.00 above the strike price still represents a loss overall. Since you can sell your options for a profit any time before the expiration date, we suggest you consider using options with longer expiration dates to give the stock more time to perform. Of course, the options markets have already considered this, and therefore, charge higher premiums for longer term options.

## Buying Call Options

The main attraction of options to sophisticated investors is the ability to leverage money. For example, if an investor wanted to buy 1000 shares of XYZ at $10 per share, the cost would be $10,000. If the stock price went up by $5, a profit of $5,000 would be made, representing 50% profit on the original investment. Alternatively, the same investor could buy 10 call contracts on XYZ, at a strike price of $12 for a premium of $1 per share. The cost to make the purchase is therefore $1000 (1/10 of the cost to buy the stock outright). Now if the stock price rises to $15, each option would be worth $3 a share since the market price is $3 above the $12 strike price. This would give the investor a $2,000 net profit because the $1 per share premium would be subtracted from the $3 per share profit. Best of all, the $2,000 profit would be made on a $1,000 investment, for a profit margin of 200%—this is 4 times the profit on the outright stock purchase. Of course, if the stock goes above the strike price anytime after the expiration date, the option expires worthless, and the entire $1,000 investment is lost. The chance of losing your entire investment with a standard stock purchase is extremely small, unless you invest in highly speculative companies. So this gets back to the risk vs. reward argument. However, we still consider purchase of call options to be a valuable consideration for investors who feel very knowledgeable about a given company. The risk is limited to the premium, and the ability to leverage investment money is extremely attractive.

## Buying Put Options

The other type of option purchase, which we would like you to consider, is the put option. This is most analogous to an insurance policy. Here, owners of long positions in a given stock may consider purchasing puts to help reduce the risk of significant price drop. For example if an investor owns 1000 shares of XYZ, currently trading at $15, he or she may wish to purchase 10 put contracts at a strike price of $14 for a premium of 50 cents per share. In this way, if the stock price slips below $14 before the expiration date, the investor maintains the right to sell all 1,000 shares at $14 before the expiration date, and is protected on the downside. Of course, the stock price must go below $13.50 before the investor benefits from the option, since the 50-cent premium is factored in. However, it is easy to see how put purchases represent an inexpensive insurance policy against market decline in cases where an investor considers the likelihood of a short-term pullback to be fairly high.

## Selling Options

Investors can also sell options on the open market. In effect they are selling these same rights to other investors. This can be a very effective way of earning income on present stock holdings, because when you sell an option you keep the premium. We must stress in the strongest possible terms that you must never sell options **uncovered**, meaning you don't physically own the shares of stock you are selling options against. This can result in nearly limitless losses for you.

However, selling **covered options** is relatively safe, and we recommend this in certain circumstances.

The sale of **covered calls** is a source of income that you should know about. An example makes this very clear. If you own 4,000 shares of XYZ you could sell 40 call contracts against those shares, and collect a premium of let's say 75 cents per share, or $3,000. If the stock price is currently $15, and the strike price of the options is $17, there is a good chance the option will expire worthless. In this case, you keep the $3,000 as income against your shares. Remember, over 70% of option contracts expire worthless, so you have a good chance of success. Even if the stock price goes above the strike price, the worst thing that will happen is that you will be forced to give up your shares at the strike price of $17. You don't lose any money, and since you still keep the premium the shares were actually sold at an effective price of $17.75. Since you sold the options when the stock was $15 per share, this still represents a handsome profit.

So, you can see that using options and short sales are more than gambling, if used appropriately. Specifically, we recommend shorting against the box to lock in capital gains until the most opportune time to exit the investment; purchasing call options to leverage stock purchases when you believe the price is likely to rise; purchasing put options to protect profits in stocks you already own; and selling covered call options to make income on stocks you are holding in long positions when you believe the market price is unlikely to rise as high as the strike price. We very cautiously recommend shorting of stocks but only when information is reliable that the stock price is likely to go down, and with appropriate safeguards such as stops and limits to control risk. All these techniques are designed for advanced investors, but are appropriate for readers of this book to know about and to consider, as they become more sophisticated.

# Step by Step Guide to Getting Started

It's great to read and learn about investing in stocks, bonds and mutual funds, but there is no benefit unless you get started. Unfortunately, the laws of inertia are very difficult to overcome for most new investors. We believe a step by step instruction works the best, since it allows you to make steady progress toward your goal without undue anxiety.

## Step 1: Make a commitment to saving.

We cannot stress the importance of this commitment strongly enough. Financial independence means that someday, through thought and sacrifice, you will be able to amass enough financial assets to live comfortably without the need to get up and go to work everyday. However, sacrifice is required to meet this goal. Most Americans are very poor savers. In fact, most of us live well above our means, using credit cards and other forms of high-cost debt to finance our toys and pleasures. In fact, personal bankruptcies are at an all time high in this country partly due to these spending habits that demonstrate little regard for the future. All you have to do is consider the fact that only 20% of today's senior citizens live above the near-poverty lifestyle afforded by Social Security to realize that it is vital to develop your own financial independence and not rely on other sources like Social Security or the equity in your home to provide a retirement income.

We implore each of you to **begin living below** your means now. By this we mean you must make a commitment to begin saving at least 10%, (even better, 12-15%) of your net income every month. How can this be done? We believe it can only be done if you have little or no opportunity to see the money. The best plan is to set up an **automatic savings program.** Your bank can help you with this by automatically diverting funds from your checking account to an investment account each time your paycheck is deposited. If this cannot be done, we ask that you consider your savings commitment to be the *first bill* you pay each month, *even before your rent or mortgage!* While this may sound crazy, we believe most people will find a way to pay their rent. It is the new stereo system or cellular phone that will have to take a back seat. With time you will learn to adjust your lifestyle, by eating out less often, or avoiding spontaneous purchases. After a while you won't even feel as if you are sacrificing anything. You will be amazed at how much money you were spending unnecessarily. For those of you who are truly just scraping by with little ability to cut current spending, it is important to hold the line on all future spending, even as your income increases. As time goes by your increased income can be used for future saving.

The key is to get started saving as soon as possible. Many of you are aware of the frequently quoted example of the 20-year-old woman who invests $10,000 in one lump sum, and never invests another single penny until retirement at age 65. She is compared to the 40-year-old man who invests $1000 per year for 25 years. Assuming the same 10% rate of return, the 20 year old ends up with more than twice as much money as the 40 year old, even though only 40% as much money was invested.

The power of time in the growth of investments cannot be emphasized enough. Starting off early, even with meager but regular investments, results in nearly exponential growth over time. To illustrate this concept, it is helpful to become familiar with **the rule of 72's.** If you divide the number 72 by the annual percentage rate of return on your investments, you can determine the number of years it will take for your money to double. For example, with an annual rate of return of 10%, an investment account will double in 7.2 years, without the need to add any additional funding. Likewise, an account with a 7.2% rate of return will double in 10 years. In the previous example, the 20 year old woman who invested $10,000 at an annual return of 10% would accumulate about $1,280,000 by the time she reached age 70, since the investment would double seven times over those 50 years. Could you imagine if she were smart enough to have invested even a small amount of additional money regularly all those years? This is not an unrealistic example, since the US stock market has enjoyed an average annual return of approximately 10% over the past 60-70 years.

These examples illustrate the simple notion that no matter how you achieve your goal, the first and most important commitment made by an investor is *to begin* the difficult but rewarding process of saving money.

## Step 2-Set up an investment account

While this may seem like a big step, it is really quite easy. All you need to do is request an account application by phone, fill it out, and mail it back with a check to open the account. Your money is deposited into a money market account, awaiting your investment instructions. We recommend a **discount broker** such as Charles Schwab or Fidelity Investments to set up a brokerage account. If you have access to the Internet there are many brokers such as E*Trade and Ameritrade that offer extremely low commissions on electronic trades. We recommend you obtain a personal financial magazine such as *Money or Smart Money* where you can read articles or check advertisements about different discount brokers. Get the 800 number of the firm of your choice and give them a call.

Schwab and most other brokers offer an entire mutual fund marketplace where no-load funds can be purchased with absolutely no cost to the investor. This type of account is ideal for dollar-cost averaging, since there are no fees to eat up your contributions. Most discount brokers require initial deposits of $5,000 to set up your account. At the same time, you can request and sign a margin agreement, so that you can trade on margin once you feel experienced enough to do so.

We prefer using a single discount broker instead of dealing directly with several different mutual fund families. A single discount broker simplifies the process by providing one monthly statement, and one location for all your money and financial services. You can trade stocks, bonds, mutual funds, and even stock options from a single brokerage account. Most brokers allow Internet access so that you can view and modify your account using your home computer, twenty-four hours a day.

## Step 3-Go to school

Now that you have made the commitment to save, have built up the excitement about becoming an informed and successful investor, and have set up your brokerage account, you need to begin learning about investments that are right for you. For nearly everyone, this will mean learning about no-load mutual funds. The first place to start is your discount broker, who can supply you with a list of funds offered in their no-transaction fee service. This list will supply performance information, management fees, and minimum purchase requirements for each fund. You can also consult some of the major financial magazines, such as *Money, Smart Money, Forbes, and Barron's*, which frequently run performance rankings on mutual funds in all major categories.

We recommend you spend a few weeks studying all these sources, before settling on a few funds that fit your personal requirements. Remember, past performance is no guarantee of future performance, so it is important not only to go back at least 3-5 years to compare performance among funds, but also to look at the stability of the fund management. Also remember to compare only funds within the same category, since there are differences in performance and risk with each type of investment objective. Once you feel comfortable with the information you have learned, try to make a personal decision on one or two no-load mutual funds in each of the following categories:

1. US Growth Fund and/or Value Fund (Large Company)
2. US aggressive growth fund (Small-Mid Sized Company)
3. US Total Stock Market Index Fund (tracks the entire US stock market, or the Wilshire 5000 Index)
4. International Stock Fund
5. Intermediate Term US Treasury Fund (average maturity 5-10 yrs)
6. Ginnie Mae (GNMA) Fund
7. High Grade Corporate Bond Fund
8. A good Diversified Bond Fund can replace Numbers 5-7

We believe it is not necessary to choose any more than 6-7 funds to get started. In fact, this is probably all you will ever need, although you may need to move money between funds, or choose new funds if your initial choices fail to meet your goals.

## Step 4-Develop your asset allocation.

As mentioned earlier, we feel this is the single most important decision you can make. Your allocation of money to different investment categories determines your growth potential, risk level, and income generation from your portfolio. Assuming you have chosen your funds wisely, your asset allocation puts your portfolio on track to reach your goals.

The critical variable in making this decision is the time horizon before you will need access to the money in your investment account. For the most part, people invest for retirement, so your current age is the best determinant of the degree of risk you can assume. However, other goals, such as a down payment on a house, college costs, or other short-term goals may place you in a more conservative position, even if you are still decades away from retirement. The longer the time horizon, the more risk you can accept, and the more money should be invested in the stock market, to maximize growth over the long term.

The first step is to take inventory of all your current finances in every account. Depending on your age and financial status, you might already have some money in savings accounts, checking accounts, IRA's, 401k plans, etc. It is necessary to include all sources of capital to your starting point. Your asset allocation is based on *all* your financial assets even though they may be spread out over many accounts. Don't include non-financial assets such as real estate, jewelry, autos, etc. Collect recent statements from every account, and then make a table dividing your current assets into the following categories:

1. US stocks or mutual funds primarily investing in US stocks
2. International stocks or funds investing primarily outside the US
3. Fixed income investments-bonds, bond funds
4. Cash-savings, CD's, money market accounts

This gives you a record of your current asset allocation in these key areas. You may generate a table that looks something like this:

## "My Current Asset Allocation"

| | | U.S. Stocks and Mutual Funds | Int'l stocks and mutual funds | Fixed Income | Cash and Money Market | Total Assets |
|---|---|---|---|---|---|---|
| | ABC Company Stock | $4,500 | | | | $4,500 |
| | XYZ Equity Fund | $8,500 | | | | $8,500 |
| | QRS Int'l Equity Fund | | $5,000 | | | $5,000 |
| | 123 US Treasury Bond Fund | | | $10,200 | | $10,200 |
| | Bank of Commerce Savings Acct. | | | | $10,000 | $10,000 |
| | Junky Bond Fund | | | $4,500 | | $4,500 |
| | Money Market Acct. | | | | $12,000 | $12,000 |
| | AAA Company Stock | $8000 | | | | $8000 |
| | Total Assets | $21,000 | $5,000 | $14,700 | $22,000 | $62,700 |
| | Total invested (excluding cash) | $21,000 | $5,000 | $14,700 | — | $40,700 |
| | Current Cash ready for investment | | | | $22,000 | $22,000 |
| | Current Asset Allocation | 52% US Stocks | 12% Int'l Stocks | 36% Fixed Income | — | 100% |

Many of you have a significant portion of your assets in cash right now. Since we don't consider cash a long-term investment we exclude the cash holdings from the asset allocation calculation. At this point we recommend leaving only about 2 month's living expenses in your cash accounts in case money is needed in a hurry. The rest and all future savings should be earmarked for investment.

The first decision you must make is your allocation into fixed income versus equities. As mentioned in Chapter 7, this will depend mostly on your age, time horizon, and tolerance for risk. We remind you that over the long term (ten years or more) most investors risk more potential income by *not* being in the stock market than by having some exposure to the equity markets of the world. For this reason, we urge you to avoid excessive conservatism. You can make an educated decision regarding your fixed income and equity allocations. A general rule of thumb is to use the following formula to determine your stock market exposure based on your age and risk level:

| *Investor Type* | *Investment Allocation in Stocks (%)* |
|---|---|
| Aggressive | 110 minus one half your age |
| Moderate | 105 minus three-quarters your age |
| Conservative | 100 minus your age |

This would place an aggressive 40-year-old with 90% in equities and 10% in fixed income. However, even a conservative 60-year-old would be expected to place 40% in the stock market. Of course, if your investment outlook were for moderate risk, like most people, your allocation would fall somewhere in between these two extremes. A moderate 40-year-old might place 75% in the stock market, for example.

Once you have determined your allocation into the stock market, the rest is simple. We recommend the following allocation for your money:

**Fixed Income Portion**
> 50% US Treasury Securities divided between an intermediate term US Treasury Fund and individual issue Treasury Notes
> 25% GNMA bond fund
> 25% High Grade Corporate Bond Fund
> (Or can place all into a Diversified Bond Fund)

**Stock Market Portion**
> 80% Mutual Funds that invest primarily in the US Stock Market
> > -60% of this money into a Total Market Index Fund
> > -40% into a combination of value, growth & aggressive growth funds
> 20% Mutual Funds that invest primarily in international stocks

## Cash

Enough to cover 1-2 months of living expenses should be deposited in a taxable or tax-free money market fund—whichever pays the highest after-tax interest.

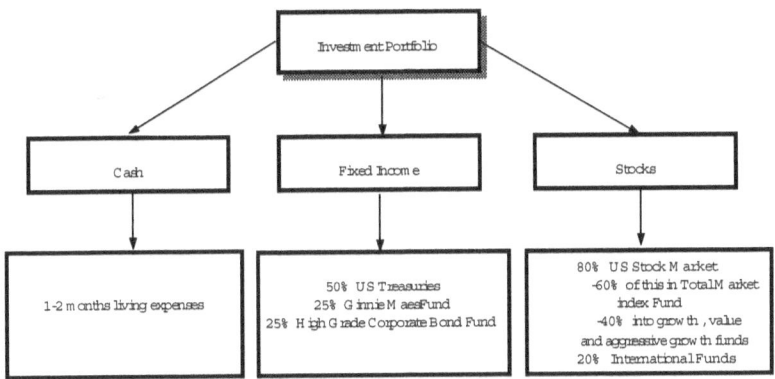

Asset Allocation model

For those of you without a current investment portfolio, with only cash assets to invest, things are relatively easy since you are working from a "blank slate." However, many of you already have some investments, and have calculated your asset allocation in the previous step. If you already closely match your planned allocation, you are ready to move forward. However, if you find yourself overweighted in stocks or bonds, you will need to modify the portfolio.

If the overweighting is in stocks you should sell off some of these assets and use the proceeds to purchase fixed income investments. Here it makes sense to unload some of the poorer performers. However, watch out for capital gains tax liability if using taxable accounts. If there is a great deal of profit, it is best to sell the stock assets in tax-favored accounts first. If the overweighting is in bonds you can liquidate some of those assets monthly over a 6-12 month horizon and purchase stock mutual funds over that period.

If you have significant cash holdings it may not be necessary to sell anything. You can use the cash to adjust your asset allocation by making purchases in the underweighted areas. For example if you are overweighted in stocks, but are sitting on a significant sum of cash, there is no need to sell any stocks. Simply use the cash to purchase fixed income investments until the portfolio is properly balanced. Unfortunately, there are so many different scenarios that it is not possible to address them all. The main thing to know is that the cornerstone of your investment program is achieving the correct allocation of your investments, even though this may take up to a year to accomplish.

## Step 5-Start Investing

Now you've already done most of the work. You have made a commitment to save and invest, opened a brokerage account with a discount broker or even an ultra low-cost on-line trading firm, researched good funds, determined your asset allocation and made proper adjustments to your allocation to fit your new plan. It is now time to start investing.

Current cash and all new savings should be invested in accordance with your asset allocation model. With current cash we recommend the immediate purchase of the fixed income investments. Since you are most interested in the income portion of this investment, you are less worried about the share price. Therefore, dollar cost averaging is not as critical with bond funds. If you are retired and current income is needed, you might decide to have the fund pay you distributions in cash. However, if current income is not immediately needed, we recommend you have all distributions re-invested, to enjoy compounding of your investment until you need the money. Also, the US Treasury Securities fund can be partially substituted with an intermediate term (5-7 year) US Treasury Note purchased either through your Treasury-Direct account, or through your discount broker.

Since the stock market portion of your portfolio is likely to be much more volatile than your fixed income investments, current cash should be dollar-cost averaged over a 12-month horizon. The idea is to avoid making a lump-sum investment at a potentially bad time, but rather to spread your investment over the average level of the market during the next year. Also, since most stock investments are made to achieve capital growth, rather than current income, you should request all distributions in stock mutual funds be re-invested to maximize growth and investment returns.

By the end of the first 12 months you should have all current cash invested in accordance with your asset allocation model. From this point on, new savings will be used to add to your portfolio. These new savings will come from your commitment to savings made in step one. Also keep in mind that all mutual funds have minimum purchase requirements, usually one or two thousand dollars each. Some investors may use all of their current cash just purchasing the five or six funds in their portfolio and will not be able to spread this money over 12 months. This is acceptable under our model. Once all of the mutual funds are purchased new savings will be invested in accordance with your allocation model.

Eighty percent of stock market money should be invested in the United States. As big fans of index funds, we recommend a full 60% of this US stock allocation be placed in a fund that tracks the entire US stock market, or the Wilshire 5000 index. We like index funds because of their low cost, tax advantages, and extreme diversification, as mentioned previously. Even better, the best known of all indices, the S&P 500, has outperformed over 70% of the actively managed stock mutual funds in the United States during the 1990's. We prefer the total market index to the S&P 500 because of the increased diversification, and the ability to incorporate the mid-cap and small-cap companies into your portfolio.

The remaining 40% of the US stock investments should be divided between the growth fund, value fund and the aggressive growth fund you chose. Here, the percentage into each depends on your investment style. Conservative investors might place more money into the large company value fund which tends to be less volatile, while more aggressive investors might prefer the growth fund, or aggressive growth fund, which gyrates more frequently, requiring a strong stomach to hold on for the ride. For moderate investors, we recommend 25% in a combination of the value and growth funds, and 15% in the aggressive growth fund.

For the 20% of stock assets allocated to international investments use a highly diversified International Stock fund of your choice. Again, we recommend dollar-cost averaging over 12 months, and re-investing all dividends and capital gains to maximize return.

We will use a few examples to summarize the all important investment process. In some cases our fictitious investor has significant current cash to invest. This is done to make the examples more illustrative. If you have more or less current cash to invest simply make the appropriate mathematical correction to determine your situation. For example, in the second example the 40-year-old investor has $100,000 to invest over the first year. If you have $20,000 to invest simply divide all of the figures by five, *but maintain the same percent allocations.*

### Example 1: An aggressive 20-year-old with $5,000 to invest, after covering short-term cash needs.

Using our rule-of-thumb formula, this investor would place 100% of investment dollars into the stock market. However, since he or she has so little current cash to invest, it will all be used for the initial purchase of the four mutual funds in the portfolio. A 12-month horizon is not practical for this investor.

| Investment Type | Asset Allocation | Investment Strategy |
|---|---|---|
| | | |
| Fixed Income | | |
| US Treasury Fund +/- Individual Treasury Notes | 0% | $0 |
| Ginnie Mae Fund | 0% | $0 |
| High Grade Corporate Bond Fund | 0% | $0 |
| | | |
| Total Fixed Income Investments | 0% | $0 |
| | | |
| Stock Market | | |
| US Total Market Index Fund | 48.0% | Buy $2,000 now |
| US Growth Fund | 20.0% | Buy $1,000 now |
| US Aggressive Growth Fund | 12.0% | Buy $1,000 now |
| International Stock Fund | 20.0% | Buy $1,000 now |
| | | |
| Total Stock Investments | 100% | All $5,000 used to make initial fund purchases |
| | | |
| Total Invested | 100% | $5,000 |

Once the funds are purchased, all new savings will be invested in accordance with the allocation model. If this investor vows to save $500 per month, 48% ($240) will go into the Total Stock Market Index Fund; 20% ($100) will go into the US Growth Fund; 12% ($60) will go into the US Aggressive Growth Fund; and 20% ($100) will go into the International Stock Fund. These percentages will remain in effect until the investor decides to change his or her allocation model due to increased age, or some other factor.

## Example 2: A 40-year-old, moderate investor with $100,000 to invest after covering short-term cash needs

Based on our rule of thumb, this investor would allocate 25% to fixed income investments and 75% to the stock market. The fixed income investments would be purchased outright, while the stock investments would be purchased on a dollar-cost averaging method over the next twelve months. The money for this would be stored in a money market account with the discount broker, and transferred through an automatic investment plan each month into the stock funds. Your broker can set this investment plan up at your request. The overall allocation of funds for this investor would be as follows:

| Investment Type | Asset Allocation | Investment Strategy |
|---|---|---|
| | | |
| Fixed Income | | |
| US Treasury Fund +/- Individual Treasury Notes | 12.5% | Buy all $12,500 now |
| Ginnie Mae Fund | 6.25% | Buy all $6,250 now |
| High Grade Corporate Bond Fund | 6.25% | Buy all $6,250 now |
| | | |
| Total Fixed Income Investments | 25.0% | $25,000 |
| | | |
| Stock Market | | |
| US Total Market Index Fund | 36.0% | Buy $3,000 per month |
| US Growth and/or Value Fund | 15.0% | Buy $1,250 per month |
| US Aggressive Growth Fund | 9.0% | Buy $750 per month |
| International Stock Fund | 15.0% | Buy $1,250 per month |
| | | |
| Total Stock Investments | 75.0% | $6,250 per month or $75,000 over 1 year |
| | | |
| Total Invested | 100% | $100,000 |
| | | |

Again it should be noted in this example that some monthly investments fall below $1000. Since most mutual funds require a $1000, or even a $2500 minimum initial investment, it may be necessary to use some of the money to open the accounts, and then divide the remaining money over the next 11 months to complete the dollar-cost averaging over the first year. Once fully invested, new savings should be invested according to the allocation model.

## Example 3: A conservative 60-year-old investor with $200,000 to invest.

Again, using our handy formula, this investor would be expected to place 40% into the stock market, and 60% into fixed income investments as follows:

| Investment Type | Asset Allocation | Investment Strategy |
|---|---|---|
| | | |
| Fixed Income | | |
| US Treasury Fund +/- Individual Treasury Notes | 30.0% | Buy all $60,000 now |
| Ginnie Mae Fund | 15.0% | Buy all $30,000 now |
| High Grade Corporate Bond Fund | 15.0% | Buy all $30,000 now |
| | | |
| Total Fixed Income Investments | 60.0% | $120,000 |
| | | |
| Stock Market | | |
| US Total Market Index Fund | 19.2% | Buy $3,200 per month |
| US Value Fund | 8.0% | Buy $1,333 per month |
| US Aggressive Growth Fund | 4.8% | Buy $800 per month |
| International Stock Fund | 8.0% | Buy $1,333 per month |
| | | |
| Total Stock Investments | 40.0% | $6667 per month or $80,000 over 1 year |
| | | |
| Total Invested | 100% | $200,000 |

Depending on individual circumstances, investors nearing retirement may not be able to continue adding further savings into the investment portfolio. Hopefully adequate savings have already occurred so that the portfolio can be amply funded and provide not only a stream of steady income through the fixed income portion, but also a hedge against inflation through the growth potential of the stock market holdings.

## Step 6-Maintaining your investments

These three examples illustrate how most investors can use a simple rule of thumb formula, combined with self-analysis to determine their investment style, and come up with a well-rounded asset allocation that translates into specific mutual fund investments. Once this is done, there is little left to do, except to reiterate your commitment to regular saving, keep learning more about investing, and maintaining your proper asset allocation. We believe an annual assessment is adequate to keep your portfolio in tip-top running order.

Since stock investments tend to grow more rapidly than fixed income, especially in a bull market, it is common for the stock market portion of a portfolio to gain in weighting over the course of a year. Therefore, each year we suggest you reassess your allocations and move money as needed to get your weightings in line with your investment plan. Also, reassess your allocations to make sure the weightings still make sense to you based on your age and time horizon. Furthermore, take a few minutes each year to study annual mutual fund reviews put out by most major investment magazines. You may discover superior performing mutual funds that better meet your investment objectives. If this is the case, and your funds have lagged in performance, do not hesitate to change funds. Remember, a few percentage points better performance over many years of investing can add up to huge differences in the end result. Therefore, it is important to continuously monitor your funds as well as their competitors in order to recognize the best performers. However, do not switch funds based on short-term performance figures. Look only at one year and three-year numbers, which have more meaning.

Also, you must monitor how future savings dollars will be invested once your current cash has been fully put to use. For example, if you pledge to save $500 or $1,000 per month, these dollars must be invested in the correct proportions to maintain your planned asset allocation. This will include money invested both in your tax favored and taxable accounts.

## Step 7-Add spice to your life

This is an optional step for investors who become very comfortable with the basics of mutual fund investing, and have amassed a considerable portfolio through hard work and dedication. To make investing more interesting, it is quite acceptable at this point to consider individual stock investing. This means allocating 10-20% of your US stock market allocation out of mutual funds and into individual stocks. Of course, this requires much more diligence on your part than just leaving the investing decisions up to a mutual fund manager. However, many investors truly embrace the challenge of researching, following and finally investing in specific companies, something they cannot otherwise do as mutual fund investors.

We recommend allocating no more than 5% of your total portfolio to any one stock. This will allow you to invest in 3 or 4 stocks, and none of them can have too hazardous an impact on your portfolio. Individual stock investing requires a high level of sophistication, as well as an understanding of the fundamentals of each company's business operations, competitors, and industry sector. You will need thorough knowledge of earnings, earnings per share, P/E ratio, etc. Fortunately much of this work can be done for you by stock analysts who report their opinions in magazines, newsletters, and on the Internet. Investing in individual stocks requires attention to detail and a willingness to follow your investments closely. It helps to have no emotional attachment to the company or its product, but to look at each investment on the basis of its merits and weaknesses. One word of caution—be careful about stock tips involving rumors of takeovers, new patents, or other news that can significantly affect a stock's price. In most cases, the news is not accurate. When it is, small investors are the last to learn of the news, and the professional traders have already taken it into account by the time you are ready to move on it. The result for most small investors is that they buy the stock at a high price only to find that the price actually drops when the news is officially announced. The take home message is that stock investing requires preparation and research-there is rarely a free ride. However, when things go well, you can gain a true sense of satisfaction in knowing your efforts paid off.

## Step 8—Bear Market Tactics

As mentioned earlier, we don't believe it is wise to hold stocks when there is strong evidence that a prolonged bear market is underway. While many people point out that any investor with a long-term outlook will do well with a buy and hold philosophy, we just can't sit back and watch our assets diminish by 20-40% without some protective strategy. This is not to say that we strongly disagree with a buy and hold strategy. Many investors favor this approach for good reasons. What we hope to do is arm you with strategies to help minimize losses, or even benefit, from a bear market.

Of course the simplest strategy is to sell all stock holdings and put a much larger percentage of your portfolio into cash. This will allow you to jump back into the market when signs indicate a recovery. The trick here is to know when to jump back in. Most investors trying to time the bottom of the market get caught watching as the market recovers quickly and they never get back in.

Another strategy to consider for investors with individual stock holdings is to purchase long term put options, giving investors the right to sell their shares at a predetermined price. The premium for these options can be considered an insurance policy against a markedly lower share price. A similar idea is to protect stock profits by shorting against the box. By short selling the same number of shares currently owned an investor holds onto profits whether the market goes up or down. In this case, the commissions and interest involved in the short sale act as insurance on the downside.

Unfortunately there is no effective way to protect profits in mutual fund holdings. Mutuals cannot be sold short, and there are no options available on these investments. However, it is possible to short major indices such as the S&P 500. The easiest way to do this is to purchase specialized mutual funds, such as the ***Rydex Ursa Fund,*** which short the S&P 500 Index. This fund, which has had a dismal record during the bull market of the 1990's, would be expected to rocket skyward in the event of a serious and prolonged downturn. Another option is to short sell the **Standard and Poor's Depository Receipts,** commonly called SPDRs or Spiders. These investments trade on the AMEX under the symbol "SPY", and act exactly like individual stocks. However, they are linked to the S&P 500 Index on a 1:10 ratio. This means that if the S&P 500 Index is at 1000, the Spiders trade at $100 per share. Trading Spiders has several advantages over index funds that track the same index. The main advantages include the ability to trade in and out of them during the same trading day, setting stops and limits on buys and sells, and the ability to purchase options or short sell them. This last benefit allows investors to make money even in a down market.

So, as much as we all hate the idea of a coming bear market, we also know that it is an inevitable part of the financial marketplace. Although economic conditions have been excellent during much of this decade, it is nearly certain that conditions will ultimately change and a bear market will result. We have shown you how to arm yourself against this inevitable circumstance. By selling stocks and putting money into cash, by purchasing put options against shares held, or by shorting against the box, investors can limit losses and protect profits in spite of a downturn in the market. Furthermore, by using more aggressive strategies, such as purchasing the *Rydex Ursa Fund,* or by shorting Spider's, investors can actually make money in a bear market. While we hope none of you will ever need to utilize these strategies, we strongly suggest you remember them, in case they may ever come in handy.

# Staying On Top of Your Investments

Now that you have made the tremendous accomplishment of setting up your investment plan, it is critical to keep track of how things are going, and get some idea of the general direction of the market in the near future. After all, you are betting your life savings and financial security on the performance of your portfolio. This requires a small amount of time and effort on your behalf. While we don't feel it is necessary to monitor the daily performance of all your investments, we do believe it is important to spend some time at least once a month tracking your progress to make sure you are meeting your investment goals. Unfortunately, books like this one are not capable of providing up-to-date information, and should be reserved only for overall planning and knowledge building. It is therefore necessary to look toward more current publications to track your investments.

There are many different sources of reference available to investors these days. These include the classic references such as newspaper business sections, financial magazines, and newsletters. Newspapers have the advantage of providing daily reports at nearly no cost. Better yet, newspapers such as the *Wall Street Journal* and the *Investor's Business Daily* provide tremendous value to investors. By reading these publications on a daily basis you can't help but become an informed investor after a few short months. It also costs very little to subscribe to one or two financial magazines which can serve as general reference sources. These publications, which usually come out monthly, feature articles written by sophisticated analysts who make recommendations about the general direction of the stock market, individual stocks and industries, as well as favorite picks in mutual funds. Also, these magazines periodically publish detailed performance and expense data on thousands of mutual funds in all different categories.

If you want more detailed and personalized financial advice, consider subscribing to one or more investment newsletters. Here, your favorite investment "guru" sends you a monthly or weekly mailing which covers the analyst's predictions and picks for best stocks or funds. There are all kinds of newsletters available. Some specialize in individual stocks; some in mutual funds; some in bonds. Others look mainly at market timing, while still others look at more esoteric subjects such as options trading, or commodity futures. Several magazines, including *Forbes*, prints an annual ranking of investment newsletters to help you determine which is best for you. While we don't believe newsletters are necessary for the average investor, we do like newsletters that focus on no-load mutual fund investing, coupled with recommendations on overall timing of the stock market. As mentioned in the previous chapter, we don't necessarily recommend a "buy and hold" strategy if the fundamentals for the overall stock market are bearish. While we do not advocate trying to time short-term corrections of 7-10%, we also see no reason to allow 25-40% of our money vanish into thin air in the event of a sustained bear market. For this reason, a good analyst, with an excellent long-term track record can be helpful in guiding investors on these major trends in the overall market. Although newsletters can be costly, in the range of $100-$200 annually, it is a small price to pay if the advice is good.

The advent of cable TV networks such as CNN, PBS, and MSNBC often carry extensive nightly business reports on weekdays, and programs featuring stock market analysts on weekends. By getting into a routine of tuning into these programs on a regular basis, a great deal of insight can be gained at no cost. Finally, the recent explosion of information and web sites on the internet represents the next great information source to investors. By "surfing" the web on a regular basis, investors can come across truly invaluable sites that provide every imaginable type of data on all kinds of investments, from real-time stock quotes, to complex technical analysis. Nearly every major brokerage house, mutual fund family, "search engine" company and major internet service provider has developed sophisticated web sites where investors go to find answers to questions they haven't even thought of asking yet. Furthermore, most of these sites provide links to other financial sites where even more information can be sought. Again, this information comes to you at no cost, or very low cost. We recommend anyone with access to a computer quickly becomes familiar with the internet. And don't forget to "bookmark" your favorite web sites for future reference.

The last suggestion in plotting your progress is to use your computer to track your investments. This means using a financial software package such as Intuit's *Quicken* or *Microsoft Money* to maintain records of each transaction and record changes in prices of your stocks and mutual funds. These programs provide sophisticated tracking tools, which monitor your portfolio's performance, capital gains, and provide charts and graphs to illustrate your progress. You will also find the software to be very helpful at tax time, since they track your cost basis, and calculate the long term and short term capital gains on investments you have sold. All in all, the effort of entering the data into your computer will be well worth it when you see how much information you can generate.

So, we urge you to use every source of information at your disposal to become an informed investor. Don't be intimidated by technology, but embrace it. Soon, you will become almost addicted to the quest for knowledge, and after a while you will develop the sophistication you always dreamed of.

# Conclusion

We thank you for purchasing and reading our book. We believe it represents a thorough but concise guided tour through the confusing world of personal investing. There are several key points which we hope you take away with you. We list them below for your daily mantra:

—Make a commitment to saving. It should be the first "bill" you pay each month. It is an investment in your future financial independence and deserves your utmost priority.

—Invest the most you can afford to in a tax-favored account, especially a company sponsored 401(k) or 403(b) plan. If you don't have access to such a plan, make the maximum investment in a deductible IRA or Roth IRA. If you are self-employed remember to open a sep-IRA plan or Keogh.

—Be wary of how you invest in taxable accounts. Try to use these accounts for purchase of investments that don't generate large amounts of taxable interest or distributions. Individual stocks or index mutual funds are excellent choices here.

—Invest only in no-load mutual funds so that all your money goes to work on your behalf. Also watch the management fees in various funds, and strongly consider index funds.

—Use a discount broker or on-line broker for all your transactions.

—Be serious about your asset allocation. Make the decision and stick with it, year after year. Review your asset allocation annually and readjust your holdings as needed.

—While it is acceptable to lump sum invest into fixed income investments, we strongly encourage dollar cost averaging all new money into the stock market.

—Don't get discouraged with short-term corrections and volatility, especially in the stock market. It is that volatility that has made stock market investing so profitable over the years. Have a long-range view.

—If you feel a true bear market is coming you can ride it out and continue dollar cost averaging into it. Ultimately you will do well. However, if you don't feel comfortable riding out an extended downturn, use some of the tactics we describe in Chapter 9.

—Don't invest more than 5% of your total assets into any single company stock. That exposure to risk is not in your best interest in the long term.

Most of all have fun investing. It is truly a wonderful feeling to have a customized portfolio working everyday on your behalf. Best of all the pride you feel in doing this yourself is intoxicating. So the next time you get an unsolicited phone call from some broker trying to sell you an annuity, heating oil contract, or stock in a Chilean gold mining company just remember to quote this book and say—***"I don't need no stinkin' stock broker."***

Good luck and good investing.

www.ingramcontent.com/pod-product-compliance
Lightning Source LLC
Chambersburg PA
CBHW030900180526
45163CB00004B/1643